HOW TO BUILD Max-Performance Chevy LT1/LT4 Engines

Myron Cottrell and Eric McClellan

CarTech®

CarTech®

CarTech®, Inc.
39966 Grand Avenue
North Branch, MN 55056
Phone: 651-277-1200 or 800-551-4754
Fax: 651-277-1203
www.cartechbooks.com

© 2012 by Myron Cottrell and Eric McClellan

All rights reserved. No part of this publication may be reproduced or utilized in any form or by any means, electronic or mechanical, including photocopying, recording, or by any information storage and retrieval system, without prior permission from the Publisher. All text, photographs, and artwork are the property of the Author unless otherwise noted or credited.

The information in this work is true and complete to the best of our knowledge. However, all information is presented without any guarantee on the part of the Author or Publisher, who also disclaim any liability incurred in connection with the use of the information.

All trademarks, trade names, model names and numbers, and other product designations referred to herein are the property of their respective owners and are used solely for identification purposes. This work is a publication of CarTech, Inc., and has not been licensed, approved, sponsored, or endorsed by any other person or entity.

Edit by Scott Parkhurst
Layout by Monica Seiberlich

ISBN 978-1-61325-246-8
Item No. SA206P

Library of Congress Cataloging-in-Publication Data

Cottrell, Myron.
  How to build max-performance Chevy LT1/LT4 engines / by Myron Cottrell & Eric McClellan.
     p. cm.
  ISBN 978-1-934709-50-4
1. Chevrolet automobile–Motors–Design and construction.
2. Chevrolet automobile–Performance. I. McClellan, Eric. II. Title.

TL215.C5C68 2012
629.25'04–dc23

2012007519

Printed in U.S.A.

Title Page: *Tighten camshaft retaining bolts to 30 ft-lbs.*

Back Cover Photos

Top Left: *Installed front water pump gear drive.*

Top Right: *This is a conventional hyperutectic piston design. Diamond boasts that its pistons are very light and still utilize a standard ring package.*

Middle Left: *Intake port view of the LT1 (left) and LT4 (right) heads. Take special note of the LT4's injector relief notch. This was originally done to create room for the injector to clear the intake port; we have yet to find any performance difference or mechanical advantage to this feature. This little notch differentiates the LT1 head and the LT4 head at a quick glance.*

Middle Right: *This is an early-style factory throttle body (left) shown next to an identical one that has been bored out to 52 mm from the stock 48 mm, and a throttle body airfoil has been added. This early style of throttle body has an adjustable TPS, which is set to .54 volt.*

Bottom Left: *LT4 (upper) intake version and the LT1 (lower) version. The difference is quite apparent.*

Bottom Right: *Head bolts are tightened in three equal steps to 70 ft-lbs with a dose of fastener assembly lube. In the approved sequence, bolts are tightened in a circular pattern. The first lap starts at 30 ft-lbs, the second lap at 50 ft-lbs, and the third onto 70 ft-lbs. A smooth, careful motion with a quality torque wrench is your best bet.*

CONTENTS

Acknowledgments 4
Introduction 5

Chapter 1: Engine Block 7
    Basic Design 7
    Year and Model Differences 10
    Desirability 11
    Upgrades and Modifications 12
    Oil Pan, Oil Pump, Pickup and Windage Tray 13

Chapter 2: Rotating Assembly 16
    Crankshaft 16
    Connecting Rods 17
    Pistons 18
    Flywheel 18
    Hub and Dampener 20

Chapter 3: Heads 22
    Valves 23
    Head Flow Data 25
    Performance Capabilities 28
    Factory Heads 28
    Aftermarket Heads 32

Chapter 4: Valvetrain 45
    Timing Chain and Cover 45
    Camshaft 46
    Lifters 46
    Pushrods 50
    Rocker Arms 50
    Valve Locks and Retainers 50
    Spring Seats 50
    Valves and Valvesprings 50

Chapter 5: Air and Fuel Management 51
    Intakes: LT1 vs. LT4 51
    Production Injectors 56
    Exhaust Headers 56
    Electronic Control Module 59
    Modes of ECU Operation 64

Chapter 6: Ignition and Electronic Controls 68
    Optispark 68
    Ignition Coil 69
    Wiring Harness 69

Chapter 7: Assembly 84
    Prepping for Assembly 84
    Bottom End Assembly 95
    Top End Assembly 110

Chapter 8: Dyno Results 118
    Build #1 Craig Nyhus 383-ci LT1 119
    Build #2 Dan Napoleone 383-ci LT4 120
    Build #3 Gary Rudolf 355 LT1 121
    Build #4 Buck Benziger 402-ci LT1 122
    Build #5 Ryan Custodio 355 LT1 Supercharged 124
    Build #6 Jim Hall 402-ci LT1 126
    Build #7 John Schaefer 383 127
    Build #8 Ron Bilyeu 409 128
    Build #9 Golen Engine Service 396-ci LT1 129
    Build #10 TPIS Intake Test Motor 130
    Build #11 Mooney LT1 392 132
    Build #12 Todd Danielson/Mooney LT1 396 133
    Build #13 368 for Bonneville Salt Flats 134

Appendix: Cylinder Head Flow Data 135
Source Guide 136

DEDICATION

To Dave Knutson, who believed in me

ACKNOWLEDGMENTS

Scott Parkhurst, my editor, for the firm push to get this book done.

Eric McClellan, my co-author for doing the nuts-and-bolts work of data gathering and great photos.

Thanks also to the folks at TPIS (Clay, Dan, Jim, and Bob) for allowing me to disturb their days for photos and specifications.

INTRODUCTION

Many say that the Gen II small-block isn't worth building anymore. Nothing could be further from the truth.

The LT1 is a smaller package and can be stuffed into places that an LS engine just won't fit. It takes advantage of a gear-driven water pump, front-mount Optispark, and the low-profile intake that was a necessity because of the new lower hood lines on the 1992 Corvette and of the 1993 Camaro. With all the years of head development, along with camshaft profiles from mild to wild, the LT1 is still a force to be reckoned with.

This book spends a little time on basic engine building techniques along with some modern assembly secrets. We also look at several different builds from tame to insane!

This book assumes that you have a basic understanding of engine building and delves into aspects of engine assembly that are beyond the novice builder. We also assume you know four-stroke theory, firing order, and that you can find the spark plug by following the wire.

History

Since the inception of the first small-block in the fall of 1954, Chevrolet has continued to make powerful and reliable pushrod V-8 engines. Despite the industry's insistence that DOHC was the wave of the future, General Motors stuck to its roots and still continues to produce the venerable engine to this day. If you're reading this, you can probably can attest to its simplicity, durability, quality, and power production.

The first V-8 General Motors produced in the modern era was the 265-ci, it went from drawing board to production in less than 15 weeks. While it only made 165 hp, it sent shockwaves through the automotive community. The 265 certainly had its shortcomings. The stilt-like engine mounts that were nothing more than really long bolts made it difficult to mount in a hot rod. (Later engines had side mounts.) The oil filtering system was less than desirable, as it was a bypass-type design that only filtered about 10 percent of the lubricant. This is a far cry from the full-flow filters of today.

Since then little has been changed of that original design. The engine went through a series of variant sizes, ranging from the initial 265 all the way to the 400-ci iteration.

The first set of big changes came when General Motors introduced its revamped small-block, the Gen II LT engine, in the 1992 Corvette. General Motors created two versions of the engine, the LT1 and the LT4. These V-8 engines were made from 1992 to 1997 in various GM platforms.

For the purposes of this book we use the terms Gen II and LT interchangeably. The engines have also been known to be called the Small-Block 2.

Design Highlights

The LT engine was more of an evolution of the small-block design than it was a total overhaul. Many aspects of the old design remained, yet many significant changes were put into service. These include tuned port-induction, reverse-flow cooling for better cooling efficiency and reduced detonation, swapping the belt-driven water pump in lieu of a

INTRODUCTION

gear-driven version, Optispark ignition system with its pancake-style, front-mounted distributor, and most notably a complete redesign of the intake manifold to a low-profile short-runner one-piece casting. One other feature is that the LT intake was dry; all coolant was in the block and heads.

A few minor changes have been introduced over the years, such as larger rod and main bearing diameters and longer cylinder bore castings.

All of these features are addressed in this book as well as a few tips and tricks to bring your LT engine to life and for you to build any power range you need!

Chapter Overview

Chapter 1 and Chapter 2 deal with the short block of the LT engine. When customers ask us to build them an engine, often times they have future plans for making even more power. The bottom end must be built for thatpurpose and we advise them to spend the extra time and money building a stout bottom end with the capability to support greater power in mind.

Chapter 3 explores the ever-expanding number of for cylinder heads. The obvious choice is an aluminum head with premium valves designed for high chamber pressure. Also, the valvesprings and retainers need to be set to compensate for the boost pressure.

Chapter 4 addresses valvetrain choices. There are a wide range of options in this department. Factory rocker arms, stud-mounted roller rockers, shaft-mounted rockers, and both hydraulic and solid roller tappets. When making a camshaft choice, you need to keep in mind that you are dealing with an intake that has short runners and a fairly large plenum.

Speaking of the intake, Chapter 5 tackles induction and how to cram as much air as possible into a naturally-aspirated LT engine. A lot of new products have come along since the last LT V-8 rolled off the line. Here, we talk about what throttle body size to use as well as how to properly size an injector for your application.

Chapter 6 discusses ignition and exhaust concerns. A few choices are available for the LT engine in the area of ignition, and each is explored including a coil-on-plug upgrade. Exhaust can be a bit tricky; we cover header size and choice and the differing types of exhaust systems and the benefits of each.

Let's face it; the sound of the whine coming from a supercharger is just plain cool. Almost everyone's plan for a new engine always includes a blower of some sort to increase the power. We cover the modifications that are specific to the LT engine to safely add boost.

Chapter 7 goes through a complete engine build of the LT. We highlight major differences and nuances that are unique to the this engine.

Finally, we dedicate Chapter 8 to documenting which parts the pros recommend to build power at any level for performance and longevity. We cover high-performance parts in various combinations to show the capabilities of the LT. The potential of the LT is tested as we go over builds ranging from stock to a full-out, high-level race engine. We have dyno comparisons in many combinations of engine size and performance. We show you how to make solid, reliable performance out of your LT engine.

CHAPTER 1

ENGINE BLOCK

The heart and soul of an engine build is the block. A solid foundation is needed at any power level, whether it is the weekend cruiser or the seasoned professional racer. The LT1/LT4 platform has a very small list of options due to its limited availability and short production run. Block preparation and bottom-end builds rarely yield more than 30 to 40 hp; we see the bottom end buildup as being more about reliability. Since power comes from the head and camshaft selection, we spend most of our time in those two main areas.

Basic Design

The basics of the LT block are fairly straightforward. It has the typical V-8 design with a few important key alterations. An unnoticed change from the older blocks to the 1982 blocks is that the L98 and LT blocks had a higher nickel content. This allows the block to be more stable; the bores stay rounder and accept moly-style rings better.

Most obvious to many old-school builders is the placement of

Front comparison of the L98 block (left) and the LT block (right).

One easy way to tell if your block has high or low nickel content is to look at the lower water jacket size. The larger hole indicates that the block has higher nickel content.

Rear profile of the LT block.

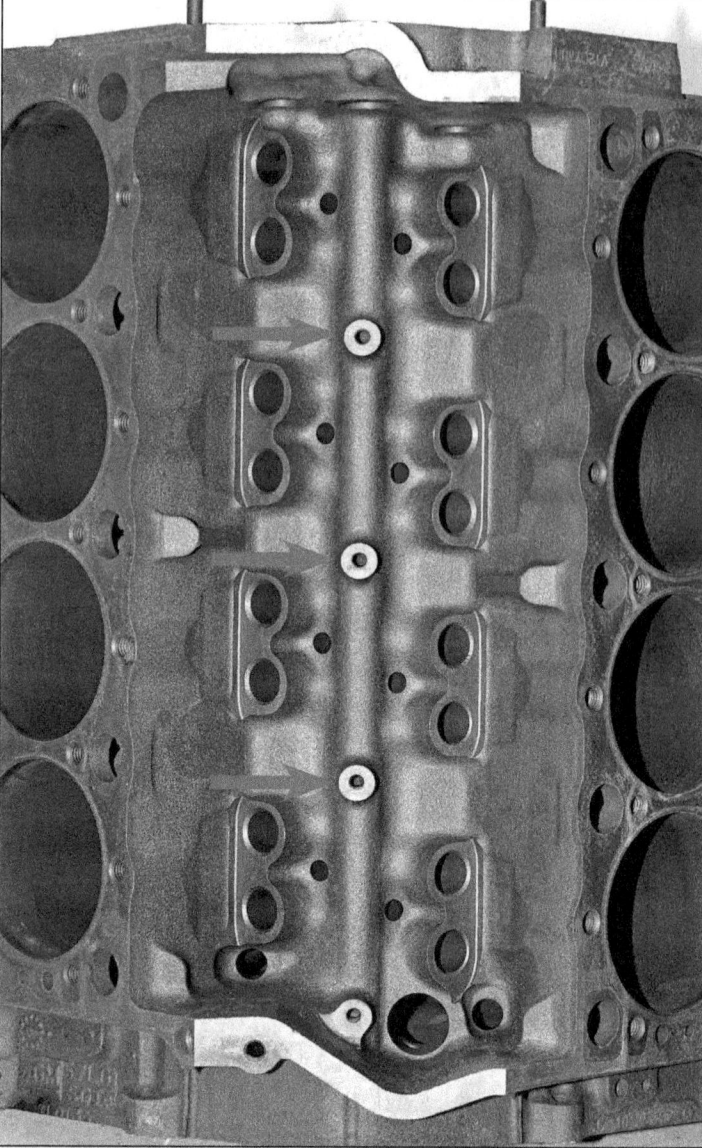

This shot shows the hold-down locations for the spider that keeps the lifters in place.

Here is the rear oil pump drive hole. If you choose to use a carburetor, this is where the distributor is installed.

ENGINE BLOCK

In both photos here, on the left is the LT version of the rear main cap with one piece rear seal. On the right is the L98 rear main cap with two-piece rear seal.

Here is the unique feature of the LT engine: the reverse cooling that flows water through the head (arrow). Be careful; although most small-block heads bolt on, that does not mean that they cool properly and could cause terminal failure of the motor.

This L98 block has no water jacket for the heads.

the distributor. The mounting hole for the distributor is at the front of the engine, oriented horizontally. It can be found in front of the timing chain cover, which is atypical of the vast majority of engines manufactured until this point.

The Gen II block features a rear oil pump "dummy" drive stub installed into the location where a typical small-block's distributor goes. This drives the oil pump. If you ever choose to throw a carburetor and conventional distributor on your LT engine, you will employ this feature of the block. This procedure requires a special intake usually found from Chevrolet Performance (PN 24502574).

The LT engine only came in two main bearing cap variations: two-bolt and four-bolt. Differences between the two for building your engine are discussed shortly. There are certain advantages to each style and we walk you through the decision process for choosing one block or the other.

Another key component to the LT engine versus the previous L98 is the reverse cooling design. The water pump is beltless and is driven via the cam gear. Don't assume that all small-blocks are equal; you cannot use any older-style short or long water pump designed with a serpentine drive system; it simply does not fit. General Motors has two basic front serpentine belt accessory drive configurations for the LT engine family: The Corvette mounts the A/C compressor high on the left side. The Camaro-Firebird mounts the A/C compressor low on the left side.

Year and Model Differences

The good news here is that you only need to memorize one number. If you are digging through the bone yard, you only have to know 10125327. That's the casting number of all LT1 and LT4 engines. It is located on the upper right rear of the block.

The bad news is that you won't be able to tell what main cap design you have until you remove the oil pan. However, here's a decent rule of thumb: If the engine was supplied from a Corvette, it most likely features four-bolt mains. If the block is from anything else, a safe bet is it's a two-bolt version. Be sure to remove the oil pan each time to determine your version because it is possible other applications were utilized. For

Front of the LT motor showing the timing cover bolt pattern. Also, note the reverse water pump drive gear hole above the camshaft (arrow).

ENGINE BLOCK

Installed front water pump gear drive.

This is why a typical SBC water pump does not work: The LT motor has two water passages; the upper feeds the heads while the lower supplies the block with coolant.

four-bolt versions, it is important to note that only the numbers-2, -3, and -4 caps feature four bolts while main bearing cap numbers-1 and -5 use two bolts.

Take special care when inspecting your block. General Motors produced a 4.3L 265-ci version of the LT engine (called L99) that carries a different casting number, which is 10168588. It also has the numbers "4.3" cast in the block itself, which makes it easy to spot as the smaller 3.74-inch-bore block. There is no real performance potential in the smaller 4.3 version, and it should be avoided or replaced with the larger LT1/LT4 5.7L engine if high performance is the goal.

Desirability

When we build LT engines for customers, we have to assess many things. First and foremost is the customer's budget and power needs. The old saying, "Speed costs money; how fast do you want to go?" is certainly true in this case. If the customer wants to make anything below 500 hp and 500 ft-lbs of torque, it is fairly safe to use the four-bolt Corvette block in the build. However, we still recommend adding steel main caps for added reliability and future growth of the customer's needs. On the other hand, if the customer already has a two-bolt version, we strong advise him to install steel main-caps on any engine making more than 400 hp and 400 ft-lbs of torque, which is very easy to do. In fact you have to make some mistakes to make less than that amount of power.

Conventional wisdom is to always use the four-bolt version of a block. In this case, it's the opposite. The two-bolt version (with

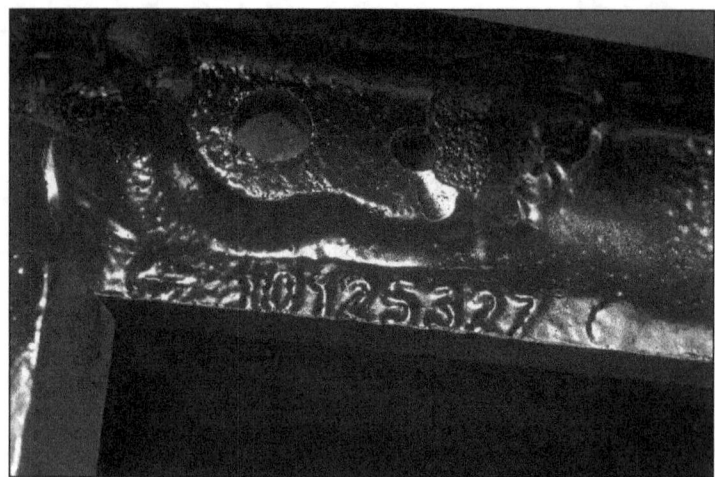
Casting number for all LT motors, found on the right rear of the engine block.

Casting date and size for LT motors, found on the left rear side of the engine block.

the splayed steel main cap upgrade modification) is vastly superior to the four-bolt version, even with the steel cap modification. The reason behind this is that the main cap bolt design is different. The factory cast has either two- or four-bolt vertical floor bolts. When the conversion is made, we drill and tap an extra set of angular main cap bolts. When this is done on the four-bolt version, the numbers-2, -3, and -4 caps end up having bolt holes not being used. This can cause stress risers and, ultimately, terminal failure. In the end, we always recommend installing the stronger steel main bearing caps.

Upgrades and Modifications

The LT block is a stout foundation for any project. Very little has to be done in the way of prep work to make a reliable and powerful engine. Typical for any engine build we do is to first clean and Magnaflux the block to check for cracks and defects. After cleaning, the next step is to sonic check the block, which determines cylinder wall thickness. The reason we do so is to check for core shift, to make sure the cylinder wall major thrust surface is thick (see Chapter 2 for explanation of major and minor thrust). The minimum wall thickness is dependent on the intended use. Standard bore blocks tend to run approximately .185-inch thickness.

We have bored a few blocks out to 4.100 inches; this leaves a .135-inch wall thickness. We only try this when the customer wants a 409-ci engine and under 500 hp. We do not race an engine of this type, as it is strictly a street application. It's important to note that the major thrust wall is no thinner than .135 inch when finished. We then deburr the block, which allows for oil to flow more easily within the block and promotes oil returning to the pan.

The most important modification we perform is the addition

The block on the left is a two-piece-seal, four-bolt-main 350; it has a left-hand dipstick. The one on the right is from an LT, which has a right-hand dipstick. Also, the caps are faintly marked from front to rear—do not mix them up.

of steel main bearing caps, which requires tapping and drilling the block to accept the angular (splayed) main cap bolts mentioned earlier.

Finally, depending on the cam selection, we may use oil restrictors for the lifter galleys. Typically this is done when using a solid roller lifter camshaft that doesn't need much oil (compared to a hydraulic lifter-equipped engine, which requires ample oil flow through the lifters to function correctly).

Other than what has been mentioned, the rest of the block preparation is typical of any other high-performance engine we build. After the main bearing caps are installed, all blocks get line bored and honed, decked (with torque plates to simulate cylinder heads), and the oil holes get tapped and chamfered.

Oil Pan, Oil Pump, Pickup and Windage Tray

We are aware of only three factory oil pan styles, and they are specific to the vehicle to which they were installed:

- F-Body 5-quart pan (Camaro/Firebird)
- Y-Body 6-quart pan (Corvette)
- B/D-Body 5-quart pan (Impala, Caprice, Roadmaster, Fleetwood)

Additionally, both Moroso and Canton offer aftermarket oil pans for LT engines. Both drag race–specific and road race–specific pans are offered. If you intend to push the limits beyond what the factory oil pan should be capable of, upgrading to an aftermarket oil pan is a good idea. In high-g situations, an aftermarket pan outfitted with a matching pickup and one-way trap doors can help ensure the engine is fed a steady stream of precious oil. If you aren't sure if your plans will ever push the car hard enough to warrant an aftermarket pan, consider it an insurance policy against oil starvation. These aftermarket pans cost several hundred dollars, but an engine rebuild after spinning bearings costs a lot more. Carefully consider your own situation, and choose your pan wisely.

A modern oil system that is designed to pull a vacuum has very little extra capacity to maintain a vacuum if you start to lose a cylinder. On the contrary, you're going build pressure because these engines are so well sealed. We install a pressure relief valve that allows anything over 2 psi to bleed off to keep from allowing the seals and gaskets from being compromised. Any more pressure than this and the seals simply won't hold, and you end up with a very big mess. This type of pressure-relief valve is available from Kinsler fuel injection. I recommend a size 8AN (1/2-inch diameter). This will give you enough volume to relieve any pressure from the crankcase. It is also important that a small filter be installed on the pressure relief valve to prevent dirt from contaminating the oil.

LT1 Applications

The LT1 was used in many various applications, from factory high-performance machines to cop cars:

Y-Body
1992–1996 Chevrolet Corvette

F-Body
1993–1997 Chevrolet Camaro Z28, B4C, and SS
1993–1997 Pontiac Firebird Formula and Trans Am

B-Body
1994–1996 Buick Roadmaster and Roadmaster Wagon
1994–1996 Chevrolet Caprice, Caprice Wagon, and Caprice Police Package
1994–1996 Chevrolet Impala SS

D-Body
1994–1996 Cadillac Fleetwood

LT4 Applications

The LT4 had a short run and was available in the following vehicles:

- 1996 Chevrolet Corvette, when equipped with a 6-speed manual transmission, including all Grand Sports (6,359 produced)
- 1997 Chevrolet Camaro SLP/LT4 SS 6-speed (100 produced)
- 1997 Pontiac Firebird SLP/LT4 Firehawk 6-speed (29 produced)

It is strongly rumored that a few police cars in New York were outfitted with the LT4 when the entire car was sent back for reconditioning.

Dry Sump Oiling

For extended-duty requirements, such as those in road racing, power boat racing, or at the Bonneville salt flats, you need an oil cooler and more than likely a dry sump oiling system. The early systems used in the 1960s and 1970s had one pressure stage and one scavenge stage (the scavenge having only slightly more capacity than the pressure side). Modern dry sump pumps are capable of pulling a vacuum in the crankcase of 10 inches or more. They also purge the air (bubbles) from the oil, so the engine sees solid oil with little or no air.

This means that you can run lower oil pressure, and your ring package can have less tension. This reduces friction and windage, thus freeing up horsepower and giving you better control of the temperature. The combination of less power loss from the oil pump (due to lower oil pressure requirements) and less friction on the piston rings (due to lower tensions) and less weight/power required from excess oil on the crankshaft adds up to a measurable horsepower gain.

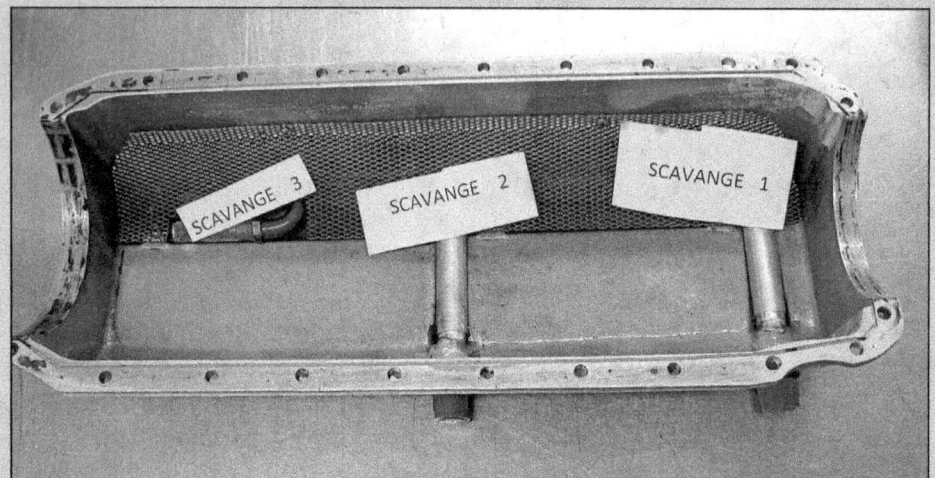

In the early days of dry sump oiling, having a cast-aluminum pan with three scavenge lines like this represented the cutting edge of race-level technology. The screen insert catches oil flying off the rotating assembly, while each of the three pickups draws oil in and supplies a belt-driven pump. The pump feeds a remote oil tank, which feeds the oil pump to the engine.

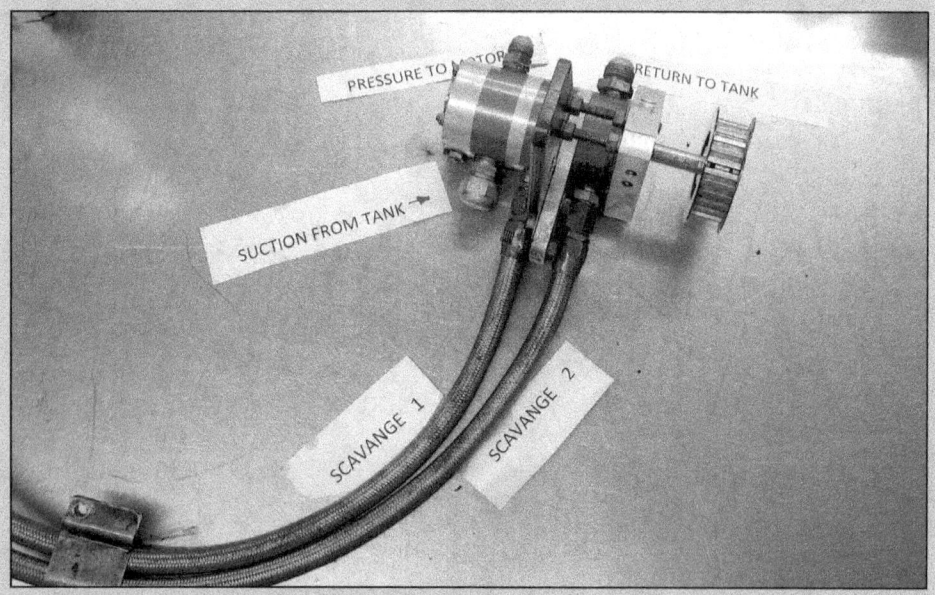

This belt-driven pump is used in conjunction with the pan. The pump provides suction to keep a remotely-mounted tank full, and also forces pressurized oil into the engine. While it can be considered superior to a factory wet sump arrangement, a dry sump setup like this is typically expensive and the multiple lines are subject to leaks. Should the drive belt fail or fly off, the engine receives no oil pressure. This is fine for a racing machine that sees maintenance between every track session, but unsuitable for a street car.

ENGINE BLOCK

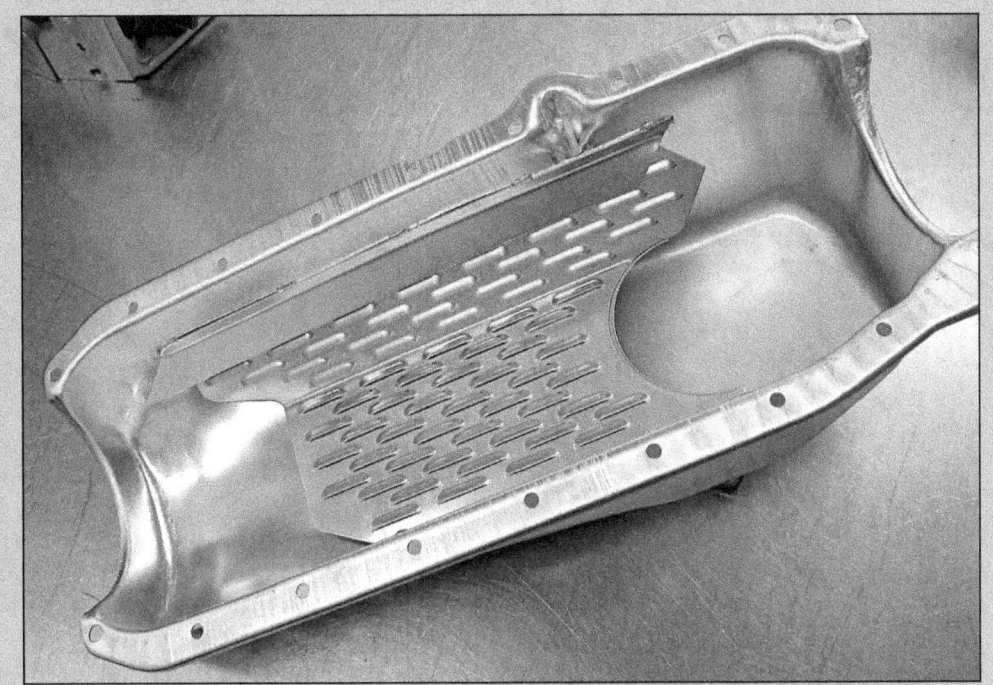

A modified wet sump pan is a more sensible choice for a street engine. The louvered sheet-metal insert serves the same purpose as the screen in a dry sump pan (to collect oil flying off the reciprocating assembly and direct it back into the pan). This also aids in keeping the oil in the tray from sloshing around too much, and helps keep the pump pickup submerged in oil at all times. This pan requires no modifications to replace the factory pan.

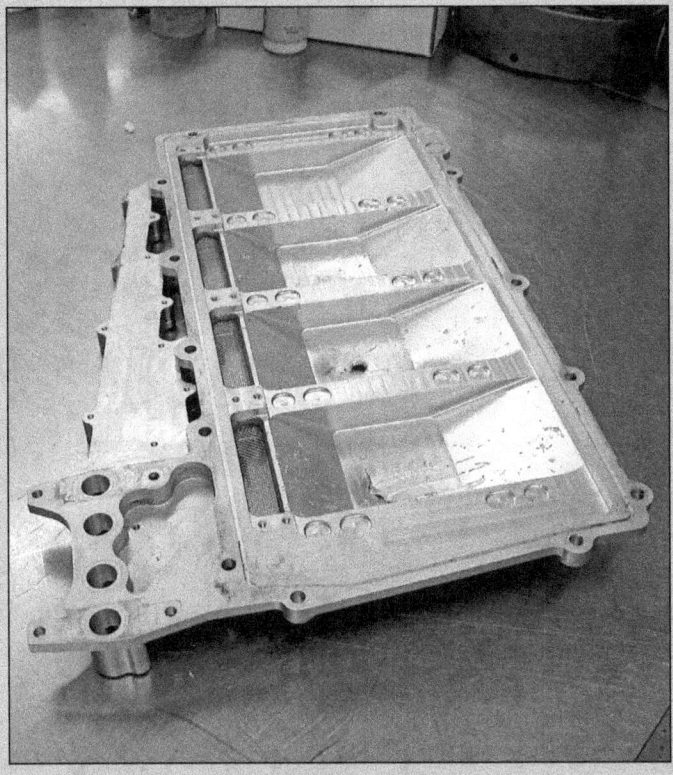

Modern dry sump pans are whittled from a solid block of billet aluminum and carefully sectioned into four distinct sumps to isolate and control oil drainage from each. This is purely race-level engineering and requires a belt-driven pump, but with more plumbing to account for additional scavenge lines. Note how shallow it is, too. The price? Several thousand dollars, so it's not a street part.

When the conversion is made to a belt-driven oil pump as part of the dry sump setup, the factory oil pump provision must be plugged. This is done with a bolt and plate secured to the factory oil pump mount on the rear main bearing cap. Additionally, modifications must be made to feed pressurized oil back into the engine. This is typically done through an adapter at the oil filter mount, or through an external oil line that is tapped directly into the main oil galley.

CHAPTER 2

ROTATING ASSEMBLY

In this chapter, we show you how to identify the basic rotating components of the LT engine. We also show you a few nuances of the LT engine compared to the L98 and the older Gen 1 small-block Chevrolet engines.

As you peruse the photos, you must realize that the factory parts are only capable of dealing with so much power before you must upgrade to better components. The weakest link is the stock connecting rod. After that, the piston is next, due to its being a cast style. The crankshaft can accept roughly 600 hp and 600 ft-lbs of torque for very brief amounts of time.

Our racing experience has shown the stock connecting rod to be the weakest point in stock form. Other typical failures are rod breakage and ring groove failure on the cast piston. Ring groove failure is usually found in nitrous and supercharged applications.

Crankshaft

There is only one casting number for the LT crankshaft: 14088526. However, it must be noted that there are two styles of crankshafts with the same casting number. The LT1-specific crankshaft has conventional radius fillets. The LT4-specific crankshaft has more desirable rolled fillets. This chapter talks more about the rolled fillet and the role it plays

The crankshaft is the basis of the engine's power production and RPM capablity.

The stock casting number for all LT crankshafts.

when completing bearing clearance checks.

Be careful not to mix and match crankshafts when reusing stock rod and piston assemblies. The LT4 version is a special nodular-iron blend, which makes it stronger. Beyond those two differences, the two crankshafts are interchangeable. Take special care to note the undesirable L99 4.3L 265-ci crankshaft casting number of 10168568, which has a stroke of only 3.00 inches.

Notice the special keyway that is used on the LT engine. Should you need to replace your LT crankshaft with a standard (pre-LT small-block Chevy) 5.7L one-piece crank, it is important to transfer the special keyway from the LT1/LT4.

Connecting Rods

General Motors used two styles of connecting rods: forged and powdered cast. The earlier versions of the LT1 had a forged rod. These were shot peened under the head and nut seat. Later in production, they utilized a powdered metal material, which the General Motors engineers felt was stronger. We have noticed this is usually the case. In fact, in mild-performance applications, these lighter-weight powdered metal connecting rods have been very reliable up to 450 hp and 450 ft-lbs.

There is a difference in weight between the two types of connecting

Left: forged rod; right: powdered metal rod. Note that both are the same length. The powdered metal rod averages 3 grams heavier, which makes the rods virtually interchangeable. However, whenever any change is made to the rotating assembly, it is always wise to rebalance the engine.

LT4 crankshaft showing the rolled fillet in the corner where the flat bearing surface transitions into the counterweight. This is where flaws are most likely, and where potential cracks can form. A more gradual radius here limits that possibility.

LT1-specific crankshaft with no rolled fillet. The more immediate change of direction increases the potential for flaws.

CHAPTER 2

The parting edge on the forged rod has a seamed line. On the powdered rod, it usually looks more finished. Typically, modern rods are still powdered metal castings, and even the new LS motors are utilizing this style of connecting rod.

rods; typically it averages roughly 3 grams, either plus or minus. This is not a hard-and-fast rule, but it is fairly accurate. It is always advisable to rebalance the entire reciprocating assembly whenever any of the rotating components (crank, rods, or pistons) are changed.

The undesirable 265-ci L99 engine's connecting rods can be identified easily because they are .240 inch longer (5.94 inches long), and have a raised dot on both sides of the beam.

Pistons

The pistons in the LT-series engines are a contemporary design, employing a typical permanent mold die-casting process with a hypereutectic alloy. It uses a common four-cut valve relief design on the top so the pistons can be used on either side of the engine and still clear the valves. It also has a common three-ring package design, consisting of two rings and a three-piece oil ring assembly (consisting of a top and bottom rail sandwiched between an expander). It is old fashioned in the sense that the rings are relatively wide (thick). A wide ring provides a good seal, but does so at the expense of higher friction levels.

Notice the balancing plates on the top and bottom of the forged rod (left) and their obvious absence on the powdered rod (right).

The production piston is a very serviceable piece for most naturally aspirated applications. Care must be taken when nitrous- and forced-induction techniques (supercharging) are added. Unfortunately, the stock components eventually fail under continued high-performance use. For instance, in SCCA road racing (in the Showroom Stock class), we have used the stock rotating assembly and won the SCCA Runoffs two years in a row. In low-power (stock class) applications like this, the factory equipment is adequate. In applications where more power is wanted or needed, piston material upgrades are highly recommended.

A wide range of quality forged pistons are readily available in the aftermarket from manufacturers such as JE, Diamond, Wiseco, Ross, Mahle, and others.

This also opens up options for different piston ring thicknesses, designs, and materials to better suit the specific application your engine will be used for.

When using nitrous oxide as a power adder, for example, you may find that the engine only holds up for a few runs. Common sense dictates that if you choose to modify the engine beyond its capabilities, you must upgrade rotating assembly components.

Flywheel

All small-block Chevrolet engines with one-piece rear main seals, which include the L98 and LT1/LT4, have external-balance counterweights installed on the flywheel. They also have a smaller center hole than engines equipped with the two-piece main seal cranks and, therefore, they are not interchangeable.

ROTATING ASSEMBLY

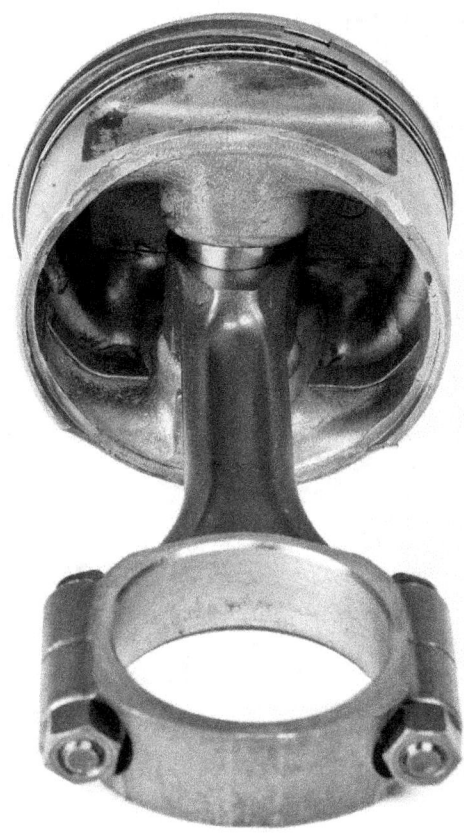

Piston and rod assembly (left); powered rod and stock piston (right).

This goes for vehicles equipped with either automatic or manual transmissions. This flywheel has the smaller diameter in the line of Chevrolet flywheels and is a 153-tooth design. It is virtually impossible to install the incorrect one.

The flywheel part number for the manual transmission is 10125379. This flywheel is externally balanced, meaning that the engine has an external balance weight on the rear and an internal balance on the front. They are made of nodular iron and weigh 28 pounds. They are very usable for stock class road racing and open track days, but they are probably not strong enough to handle repeated drag racing use. For drag racing, an upgrade to a higher-quality flywheel is recommended, and choosing one that has been certified by SFI for competition use is an assurance of high quality and improved safety.

Here's a comparison of LT pistons from Diamond Pistons. The piston on the left is used on supercharged applications; notice the dished cap. The piston on the right is a conventional hyperutectic design. Diamond boasts that its pistons are very light and still utilize a standard ring package.

These photos show the difference between a one-piece rear-seal 350-ci small-block flywheel that has counter weight added to it (left, circle) and a two-piece rear-seal flywheel that does not have a counter weight (right). Also, note the larger-diameter crankshaft center hole on the two-piece version.

All the major aftermarket clutch manufacturers (including Centerforce, Hays, McLeod, and others) offer SFI-rated flywheels for the LT engines. Flywheel manufacturer Fidanza also offers upgraded aluminum LT products.

Hub and Dampener

The LT-series engine's hub and dampener are significantly different than on the conventional 350-ci Chevrolet small-block V-8. First and foremost is the addition of a separate hub, which is a departure from convention. The hub and dampener are indexed to each other; the larger hump on the hub mates to the dampener's triangle-shaped nub. The bolt pattern is also designed to ensure correct installation.

There is also a difference between the Corvette and Camaro LT dampeners. The belt is aligned differently and must be double-checked before installing the dampener. Naturally, this is dependent upon whether you are using the Corvette or Camaro belt-driven accessory drive.

The hub has no keyway cut into it, so you must use a special key to make it fit properly. We usually

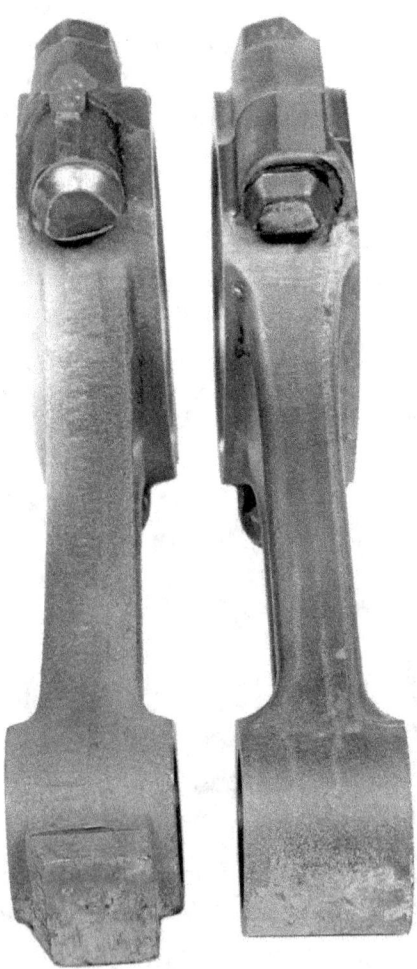

Left: L98 stock replacement harmonic balancer; right: LT specific harmonic balancer. Note that the two are not interchangeable.

ROTATING ASSEMBLY

Differences between offsets on the LT dampeners.

This photo shows the stepped keyway that is unique to the LT motor. Failure to pay attention to this detail can result in splitting the hub during reassembly unless you broach the keyway.

LT-specific crankshaft hub to mount balancer.

do this on high-performance and supercharged applications. The reason we install a keyway onto the hub and mark the dampener is to be able to provide the necessary top dead center for aftermarket engine management systems, such as FAST, MOTEC, EFI Tech, Accel, Holley, etc.

Again, if you intend to really push your engine (making more than 500 hp or in competition) it's recommended you step up to a high-quality aftermarket dampener. These too are certified by SFI for competition use, and the experts at ATI have several different models available in steel and aluminum.

CHAPTER 3

HEADS

We often get the question, "What is the real difference between the LT1 and the LT4?" The simplest and most accurate answer is the cylinder heads. You might say that the LT4 had a different intake, but that's where you'd be wrong. The only difference between the two induction systems is that the LT4 intake is painted red. We've done the testing and the data doesn't lie.

We've also done extensive research to ensure that the LT engines we build make as much power as possible, and make it reliably. Common wisdom suggests that any significant power gains from an engine versus the factory offering are typically from the cylinder heads, and that is no different for the LT series of engines.

Older (first generation) small-block Chevy cylinder heads do not fit the Gen II engine. This is due to the reverse-flow cooling design and the special water jacket.

Be aware that the 265-ci L99 cylinder head cannot be used on the 350-ci block due to the smaller combustion chamber volume. The LT4 head has a smaller 54-cc combustion

Comparison of the LT1 (left) and LT4 (right) head.

HEADS

LT1/LT4 Cylinder Head Casting Numbers

There were several different cylinder heads made for the LT1 series of engines:

Head	PN
LT1 Cast Iron from 1992–1993	12554290
LT1 Cast Iron from 1994–1997	10125320
LT1 Aluminum	10128374
LT4 Aluminum	10208890
1996 Corvette	12363287
265-ci L99 Cast Iron	10168568

LT1 intake port height is shown here, roughly .6 inch.

LT4 head with the intake port showing a much lower height at .3 inch. This is due to the engineers at General Motors raising the volume of the port for more fuel and air.

LT4 casting number 12555690.

chamber to help it achieve a 10.8:1 compression ratio, which was slightly bumped up from the LT1s 10.5:1.

Other differences among older-generation small-block Chevy heads versus the LT heads include the bolt spacing for mounting the intake manifold. All Gen II heads have this feature to allow the heads to be used with intakes specially designed for use with the LT series; the bolt angle is also very different. Also, it must be noted that the LT head does not contain a crossover cooling passage for the intake.

LT4 rocker studs are a much larger 7/16-inch-diameter screw-in style, while the LT1 has a 3/8-inch-diameter stud. The advantage of this is that it stiffens the valvetrain, which gives a crisper valve action.

It goes without saying that if the cylinder heads are not interchangeable, then the head gaskets are not interchangeable either. Once again, this is due to the reverse-cooling layout. They look very similar to standard first-generation (265 to 400 ci) small-block Chevy head gaskets, but are exclusive to the LT engine.

Valves

The LT4 had sodium-filled hollow-stem valves, while the LT1 valves were solid. The LT4 was a departure from the solid-stemmed valve found in conventional small-block Chevrolet engines until this point.

All LTs share the same valvespring, but there is a difference in the weight of the valves. The LT4's hollow-stem valves weigh 30 grams less than the solid valves in the LT1. The weight of all the objects on the rocker side of the stud of the valvetrain are crucial, especially at higher RPM levels. The weight of the

CHAPTER 3

The LT4 head is cast with a mark to distinguish it from the LT1 head. This can help you identify the motor more quickly if you are rummaging through the junkyard.

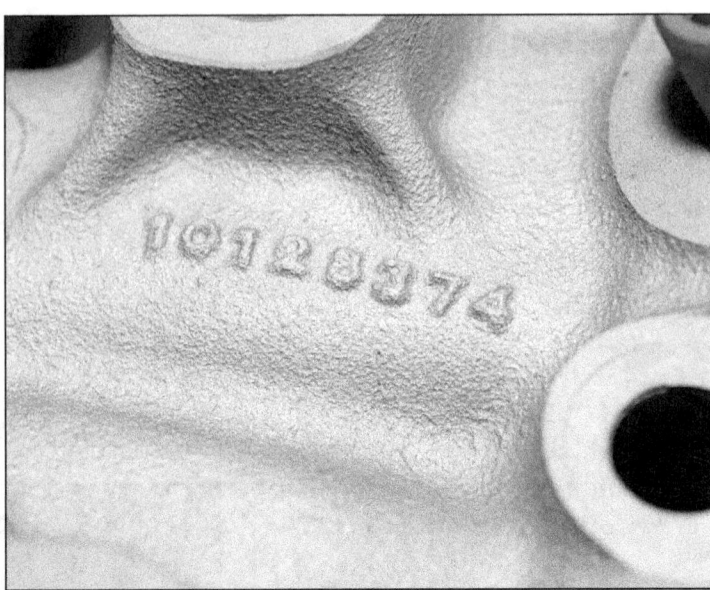

LT1 casting number 10128374.

These exhaust ports are CNC-finished to a tight standard.

pushrod doesn't seem to make much difference in the RPM capability of the engine.

We experimented with rev kits early in the LT1 production cycle and they seemed to make very little difference in power, durability, or wear. However, other high-performance engine builders have seen power gains after the addition of a rev kit. One possible explanation for this is that they may be running camshaft lobes with extremely fast ramps. Such cams can have "stutter points" where the lifter isn't moving up the ramp smoothly, and if this is the case, a rev kit could be advantageous.

The valves in the LT4 heads are the kind of part that you would find in a premium street race engine. Besides the hollow stem, they are back cut and scoop milled on the heads. Their prices reflect this, as the current cost for an LT1 intake valve is around $20, while the LT1 exhaust valve is about $25. On the other hand, the LT4 intake valve costs something like $34 while the LT4 exhaust valve is around $50.

So the question is, at almost double the price, are they worth it? Let's examine the weight difference. The LT1 intake weighs 113 grams versus the LT4 at 84 grams. The LT1 exhaust weighs 95 grams versus the LT4 at 73.5 grams. The weight loss on the exhaust valve is most important because the piston chases the closing valve up the bore on the exhaust stroke. With the heavier valve, the spring can lose control and the result is valve float. This can result in a major engine failure if the piston makes contact with the valve.

The next step up in weight savings is a titanium valve. Today, these cost between $125 and $175 per valve, so it is not an upgrade for everyone. If your needs can justify the expense, titanium valves represent a genuine weight savings in the valvetrain and will contribute to longer valvespring life as a result. This upgrade is quantifiable enough that even some OEM high-performance vehicles (like the new Corvette) now ship with titanium valves.

One other item unique to the LT/4 is the rocker stud and aluminum

HEADS

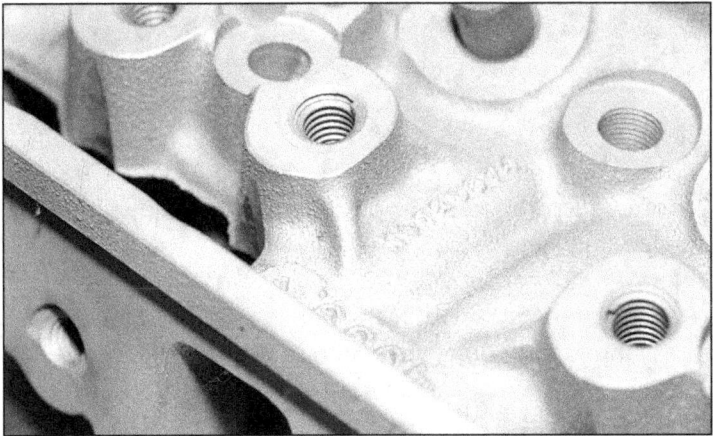

The LT1 head has a rocker stud boss that stands taller than the LT4 head, because of the lower port roof height. We have assumed that the original engineering of the motor must have had a high failure rate of this component, which is why we think the engineers felt the need to add the extra bracing.

The LT4 port roof height is significantly higher than the LT1 and, therefore, does not need the extra bracing of the rocker stud boss.

rocker arm. The rocker arm carries a 1.6:1 ratio, compared to the standard 1.5:1 common to all other Chevy small-blocks up to and including the LT1. It is also nonadjustable beyond standard preload (lash) settings. If you change the camshaft, make sure the pushrods are still the correct length.

Head Flow Data

There are many choices for cylinder heads in the market today, and something for anyone's budget. In the Appendix on page 127 there are 22 airflow tests. The flow bench data was collected on a Super Flow 300 bench at the industry-standard 28 inches of water. The casting numbers listed are the last three digits of the factory head casting number. We hope this chart saves you some time. It shows the progression of port design from the L98 to the LT engine.

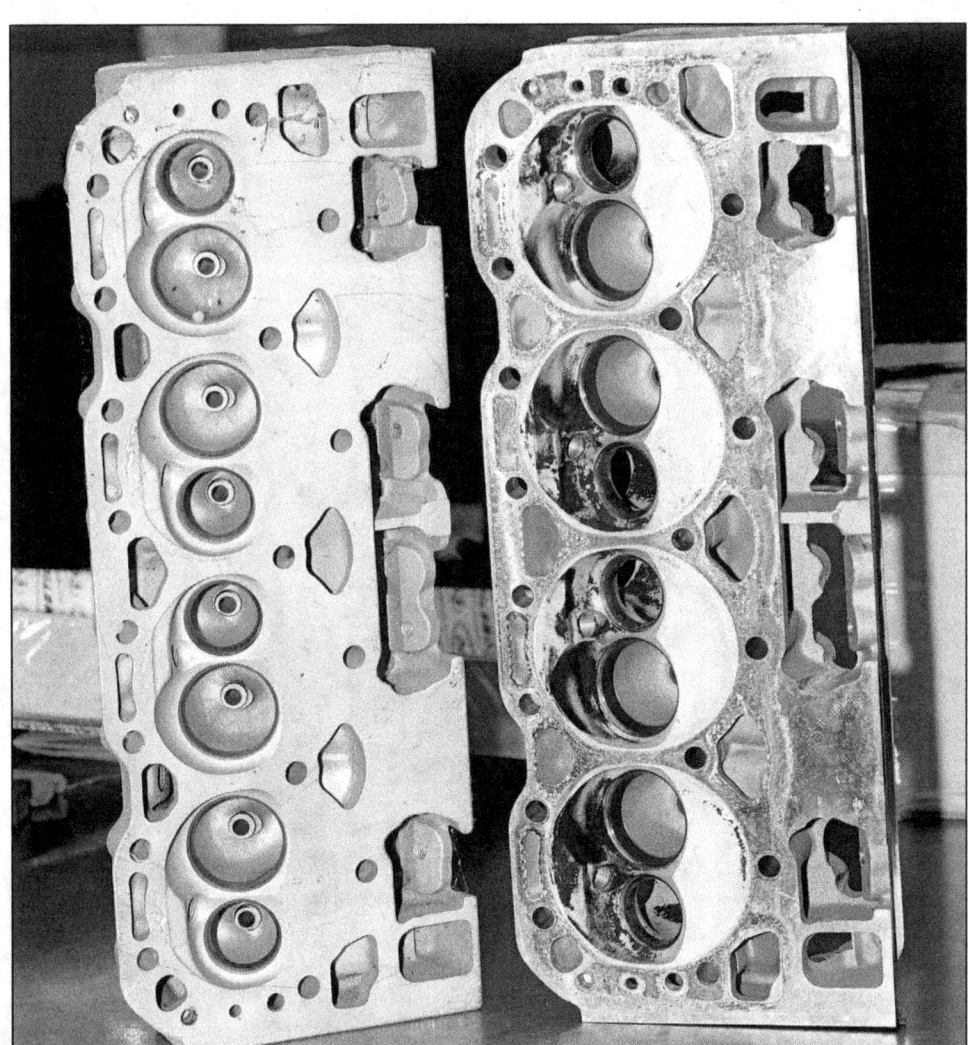

Comparison of the LT1 (left) and LT4 (right) combustion chambers.

Cooling System Design

One of the LT engine's defining characteristics is its cooling system design. Beyond its reverse-rotation water pump, the cylinder heads are the clearest engineering departure from the traditional small-block Chevy architecture.

The basic design difference is that the coolant is routed from the radiator through the cylinder heads first, and then through the engine block. This is just the opposite sequence from the traditional small-block. The reason for this change is simple: by pumping cooler water through the heads first, more heat is removed from the heads. This means the heads can deal with more heat, since more heat is being removed from them.

Cooler cylinder heads are less likely to detonate when faced with low-octane gasoline and higher compression ratios as compared to hotter heads, or heads that are cooled less efficiently. For this reason, LT-series engines can run higher compression ratios than comparable first-generation small-block Chevy engines, especially small-blocks with iron heads. The aluminum heads of the LT transfer heat more readily than cast iron, so when teamed with the revised cooling system design, the difference becomes even more dramatic.

What did not change in the evolutionary step from the traditional (since 1955) small-block Chevy to the LT series was the rest of the engine's basic architecture. Any previous small-block head physically bolts into place, since none of the head bolts or spacing was moved in the transi-

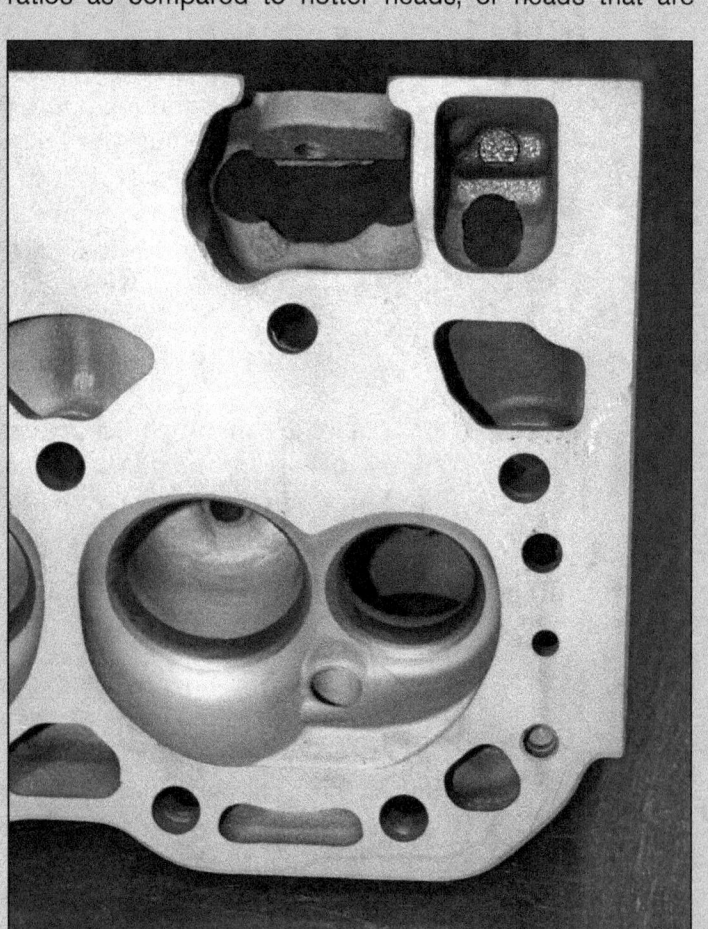

We've placed a traditional small-block head (above) alongside an LT-series cylinder head (left) to show the differences. If we look at the LT head, the coolant pathways in the upper right-hand corner are clear.

HEADS

tion to LT status. This means it's possible for traditional small-block heads to be modified for use on LT engines if the cooling passages are appropriately moved. This process involves the plugging of some passages and the addition of others.

The traditional passageways across the front and rear of the head are eliminated and instead are re-routed down into the head.

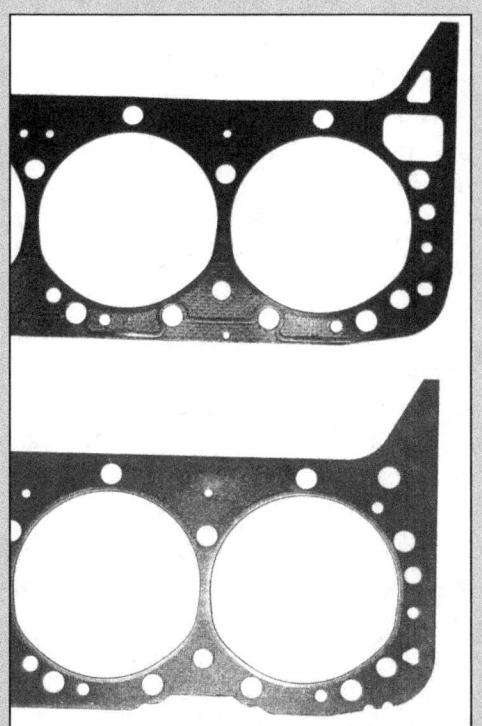

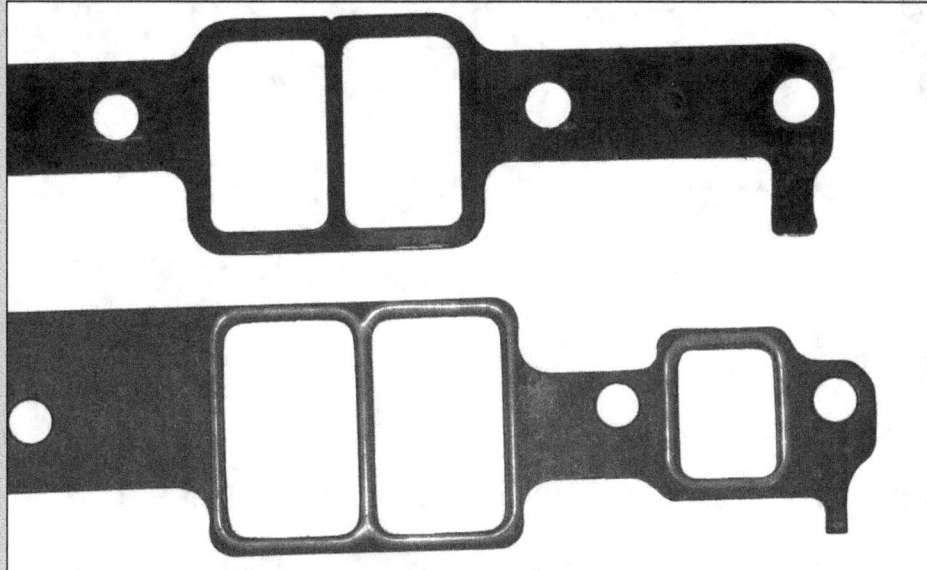

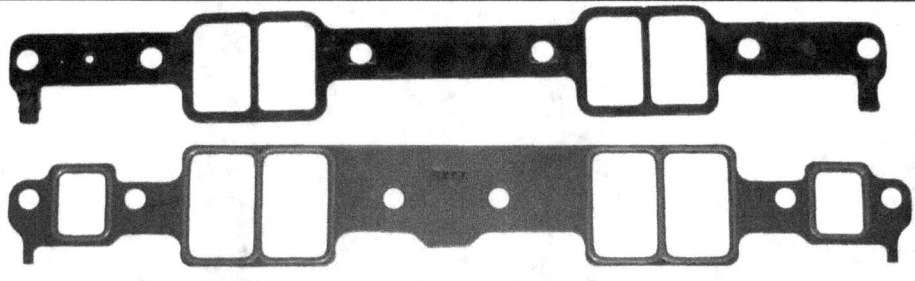

This also means different gaskets are required for both the intake manifold-to-head surface and the cylinder head-to-block surface to account for the change in coolant routing. When we compare traditional first-generation small-block intake gaskets (bottom) to the LT-specific intake gaskets (top) the elimination of the coolant passages across the front and rear of the intake are clearly seen.

Finally, the addition of a coolant path from the head to the block is clear in the head gasket as well. The upper gasket clearly has provision for the additional coolant path, while the lower gasket does not. The potential for modified heads to be used in LT applications means that any small-block Chevy cylinder head could be used on an LT-Series application if these upgrades are accomplished. They are not prohibitively expensive, but the costs must be accounted for when comparing non-LT aftermarket performance heads to those designed to be simply bolted-on to the LT engines. Our recommendation is to stick with the LT designs if they are compatible with your engine's goals, and only pay for the required mods if a suitable LT-specific head cannot be found.

Intake port view of the LT1 (left) and LT4 (right) heads. Take special note of the LT4's injector relief notch. This was originally done to create room for the injector to clear the intake port; we have yet to find any performance difference or mechanical advantage to this feature. This little notch differentiates the LT1 head and the LT4 head at a quick glance.

Performance Capabilities

If you are on a tight budget when building your LT-based engine, you may be thinking of porting and polishing your own cylinder heads (see Chapter 6 for more information).

The end result of the factory cylinder head's ability to remain in service has to do with how carefully you tune the engine and how much compression you throw at it. The factory LT heads do not have enough deck thickness for ample nitrous injection or serious supercharging. If they did, it would inevitably lead to head gasket failures, at a minimum. For a normally aspirated street engine on pump gas, we would limit the compression ratio to 11:1.

Factory Heads

The factory cylinder heads for the LT-series engines were relatively good. They were cast out of aluminum, which was still a pretty big deal at the time. They had decent port design and well-designed chambers that offered efficient burn characteristics. With a little time invested in porting and chamber shaping, the factory LT1 and LT4 heads could be made even better, and some excellent horsepower and torque has been made by engines using modified versions of these factory heads.

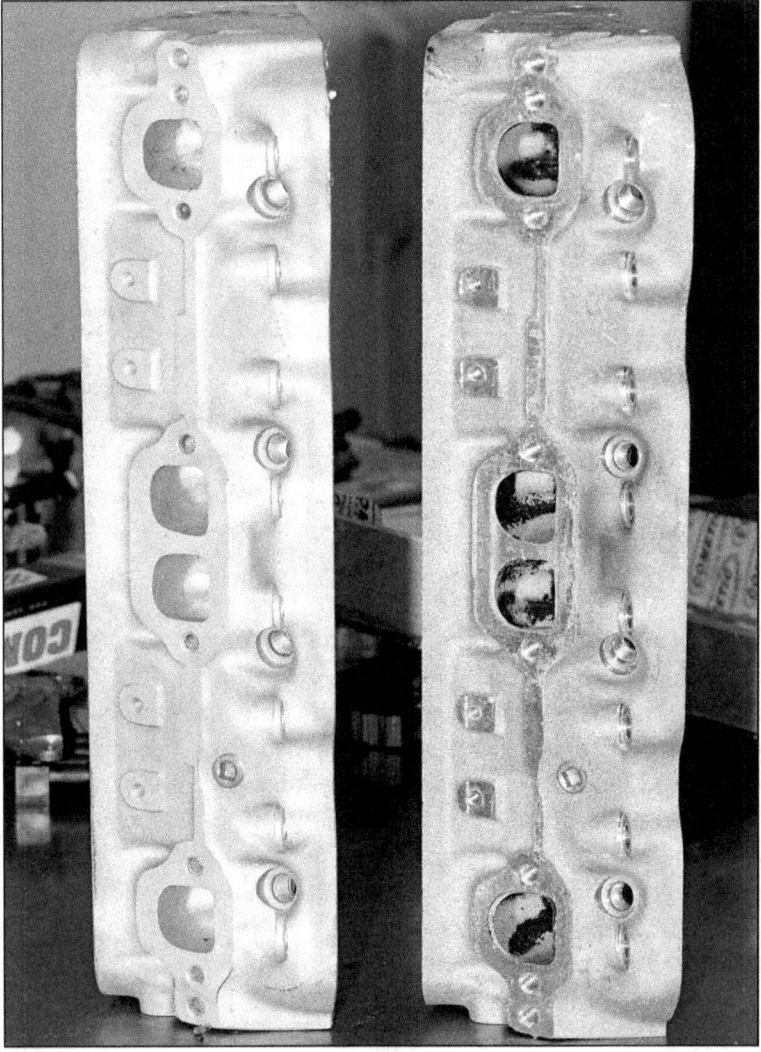

Exhaust port view of the LT1 (left) and LT4 (right) heads. The exhaust port size is exactly the same and no differences can be found here.

HEADS

Factory Heads

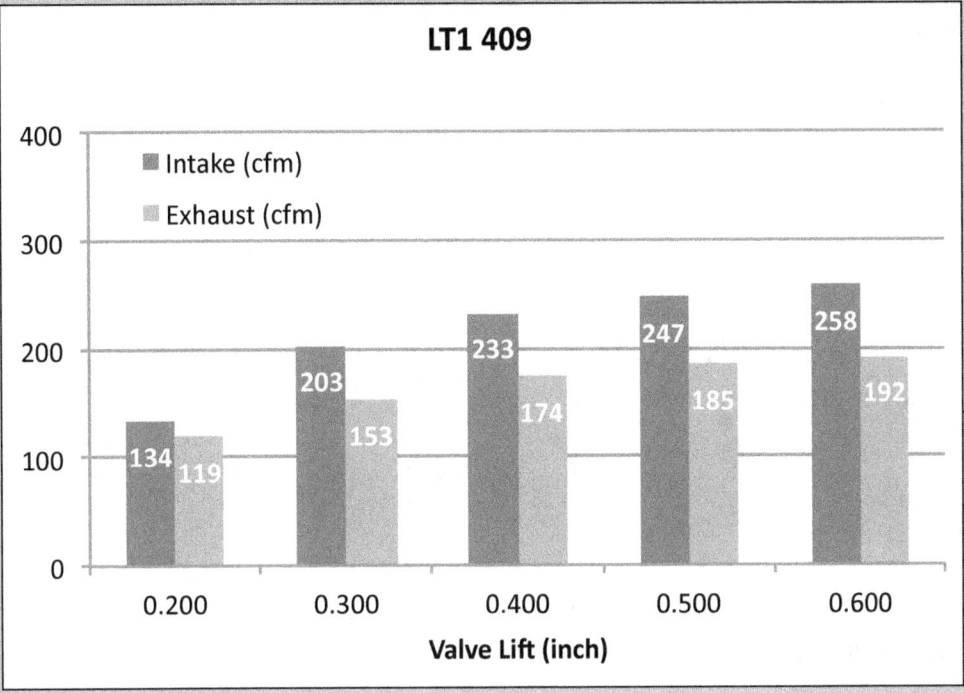

LT1 409

Valve Lift (inch)	Intake (cfm)	Exhaust (cfm)
0.200	134	119
0.300	203	153
0.400	233	174
0.500	247	185
0.600	258	192

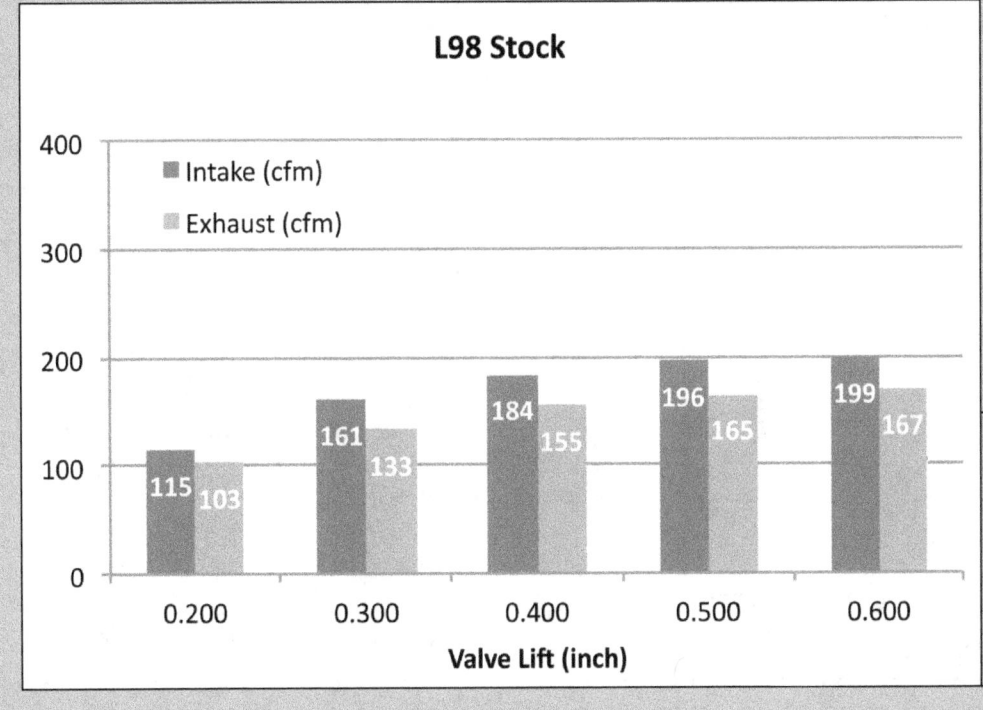

L98 Stock

Valve Lift (inch)	Intake (cfm)	Exhaust (cfm)
0.200	115	103
0.300	161	133
0.400	184	155
0.500	196	165
0.600	199	167

Factory Heads CONTINUED

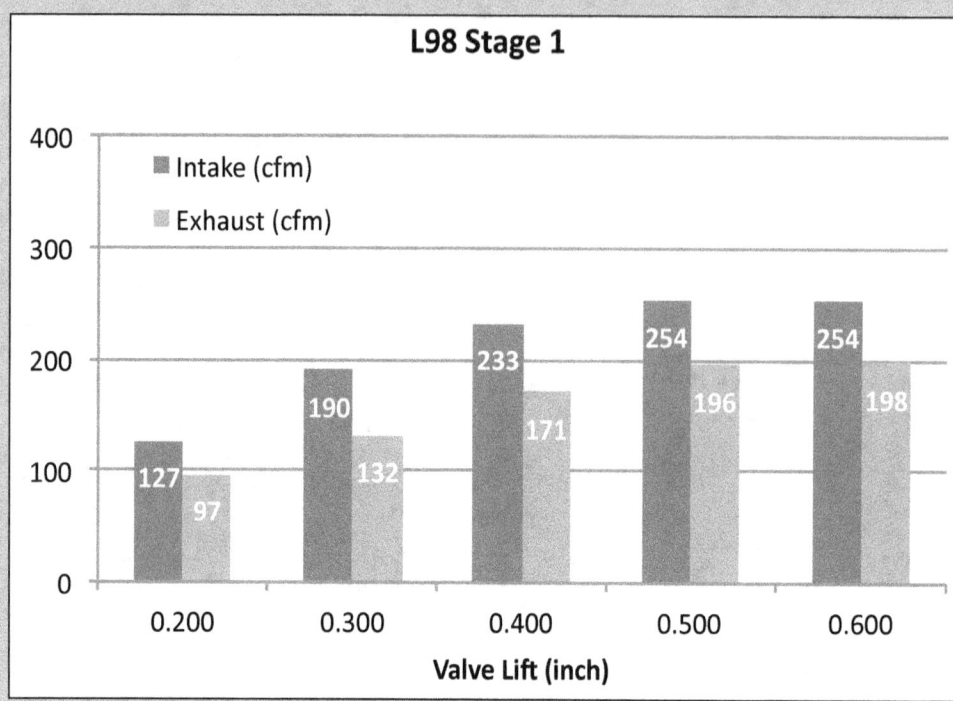

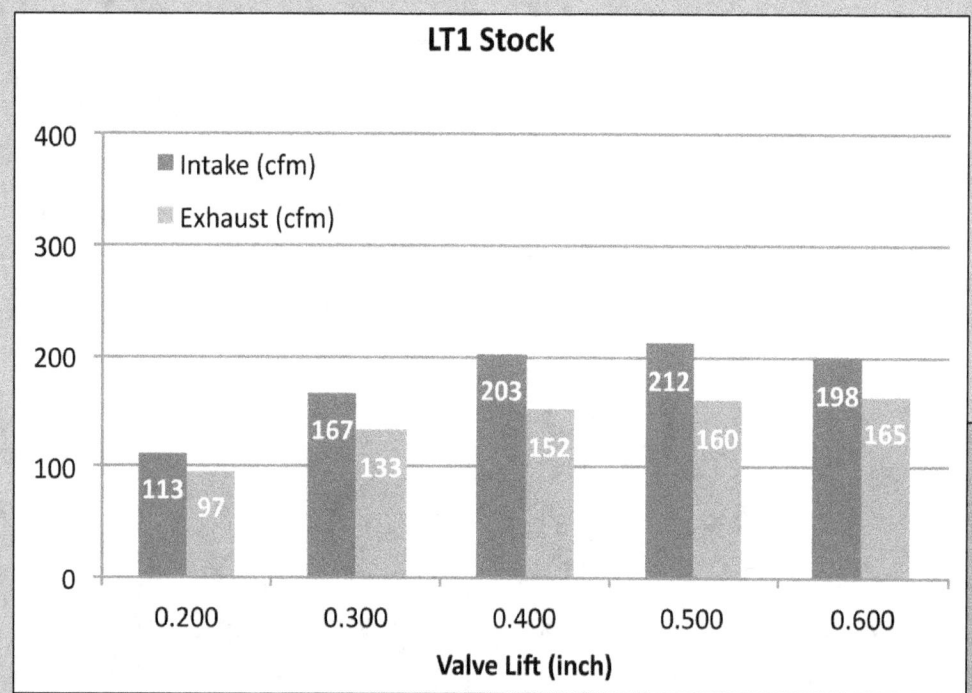

HEADS

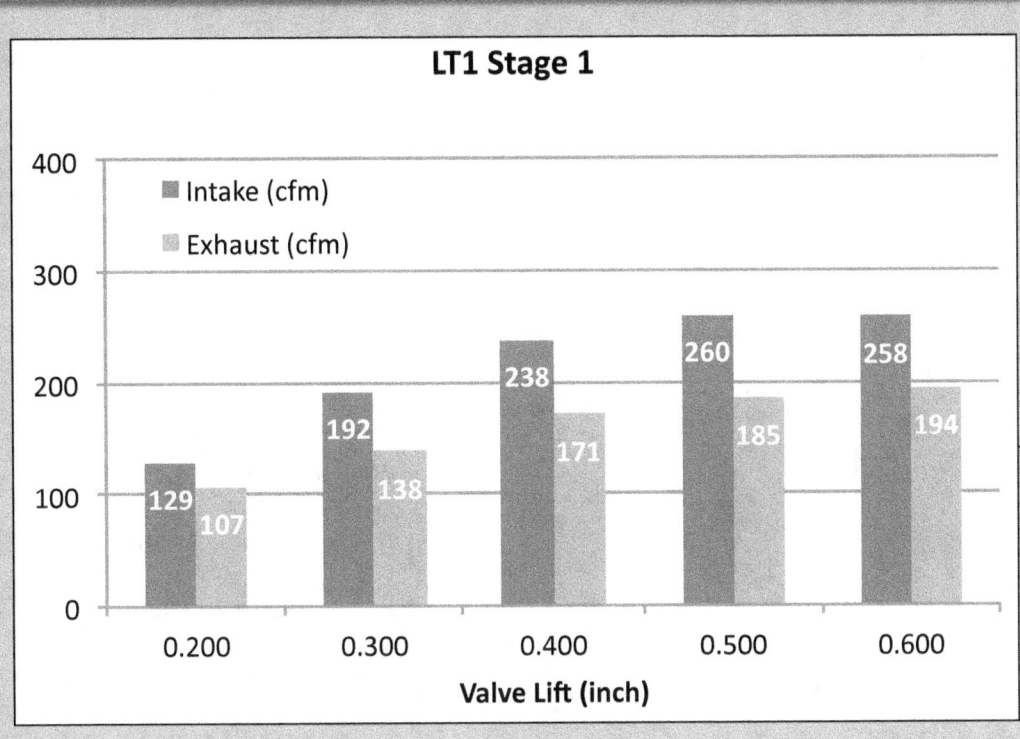

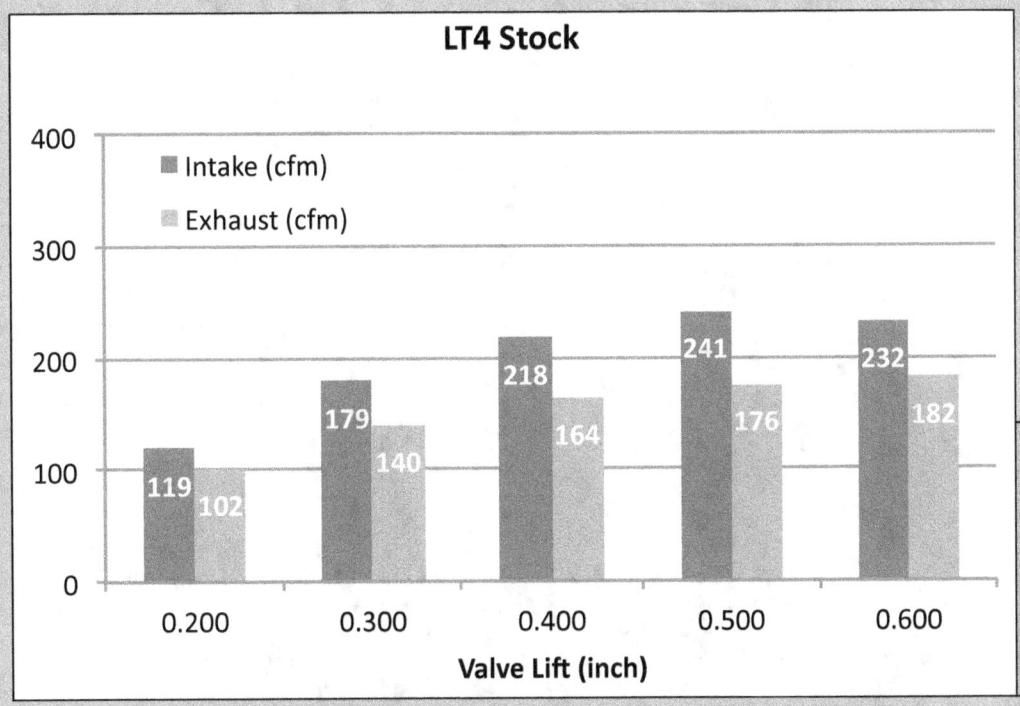

Factory Heads CONTINUED

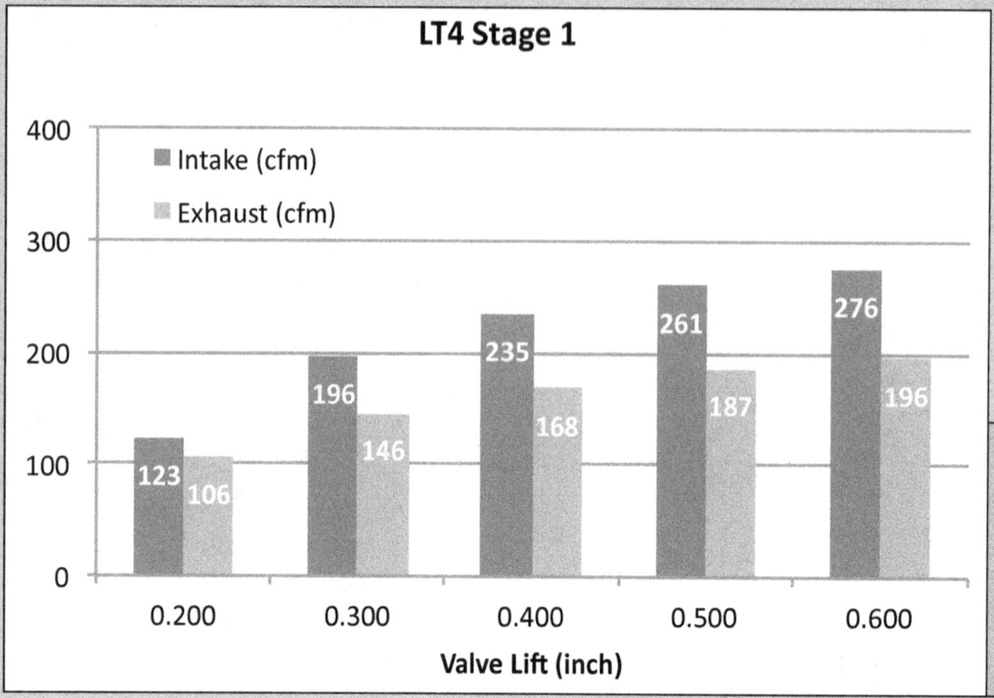

LT4 Stage 1

Valve Lift (inch)	Intake (cfm)	Exhaust (cfm)
0.200	123	106
0.300	196	146
0.400	235	168
0.500	261	187
0.600	276	196

Aftermarket Heads

As with any engine coveted by power-hungry enthusiasts, the market existed for a clean-sheet high-performance cylinder head that was engineered purely for performance atop the popular LT short block. Thousands of Camaro/Firebird, Corvette, and Impala SS/Caprice owners were willing to drop the dollars. The LT engine's similarity to the traditional first-generation small-block Chevy meant existing tooling could be used. Certainly the existing small-block Chevy aftermarket heads could be used as models, and with the necessary modifications, LT heads could be offered with solid performance without having to reinvent the wheel.

All of the traditional big players in the cylinder head aftermarket offer

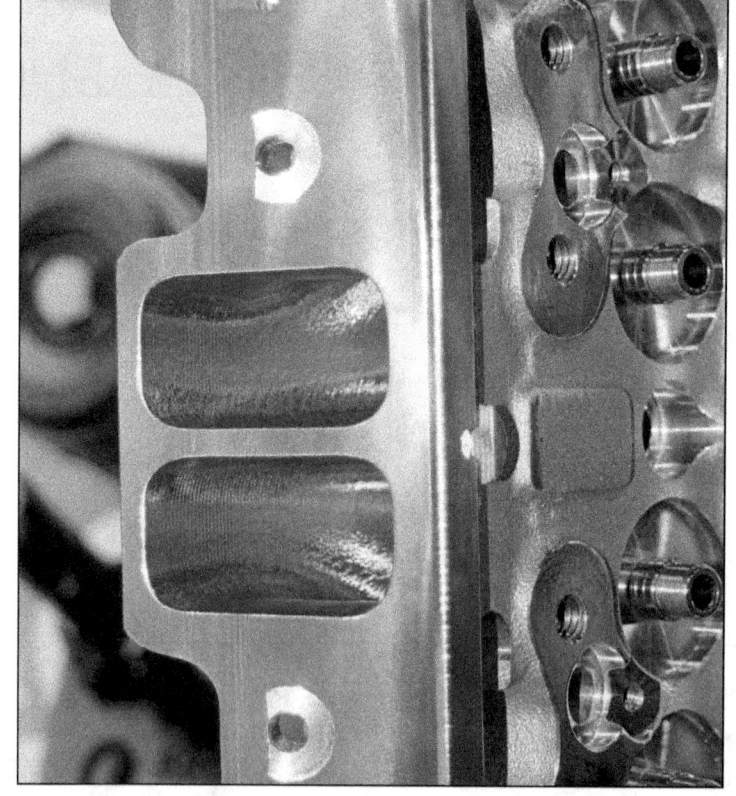

The intake and exhaust ports shown here are all Eliminator castings. AFR offers several valve-spring options to match the rest of your engine design. If you do your homework, you should be able to bolt on the heads, right out of the box (after a mandatory cleaning, of course).

HEADS

an LT-specific head (or two). These heads all boast thicker deck surfaces, revised and improved port designs, nice chambers, and oversized valves. If you're looking at building a serious LT-based engine for competition, you have choices. They're all good, and by comparing the specifics of each one, you should be able to decide which one best suits your particular project's needs.

Air Flow Research (AFR)

Valencia, California–based AFR offers the widest selection of heads for LT engines, with four different part numbers currently in stock and options that push the number of available heads to more than ten. You can choose from straight or angled spark plugs, 55- or 65-cc combustion chambers, and some other extra-cost options such as angle milling or the additional machining required to run cams over .600-inch lift. The intake port volumes offered by AFR include 180, 195, 210, and 227 cc. Unless you request otherwise, all the ports and chambers are CNC-finished so they are identical to each other and offer ideal performance based on AFR's research. All AFR heads also come with a competition five-angle valve job, which is really nice.

The 227-cc model is worthy of mention on its own. This head represents the upper end of commercially available heads for LT engines and it brings with it some special requirements. Combustion chamber volume choices are 65 or 75 cc, and large-diameter 2.1-inch (intake) and 1.6-inch (exhaust) valves come standard. Offset stud girdles are required, since AFR had to alter the factory valve location by offsetting the intake valve .050 inch to get those wider valves in there. These offset matching girdles are available from AFR, of course. Two different exhaust port configurations are also offered: a standard (factory) port location and a spread-port design. In both cases, the exhaust ports have been raised .250 inch higher than factory to improve flow, so exhaust system considerations must be made since some header clearances may be affected depending on the header and chassis.

Because of the offset intake valve design, the intake rocker arm is at a slight angle and the rocker arm's roller tip is not perfectly parallel on the valve tip. It is not perfectly centered on the valve tip either. While this doesn't have any significant effect on power production, it requires regular inspection to ensure nothing bad happens between the rocker's roller tip and the top of the valve. It's because of this design variance that these heads aren't recommended for street use.

On the other end of the spectrum, AFR's 180- and 195-cc heads carry a California emissions Exemption Order (E.O.) number, which means they are completely legal for use on vehicles with smog controls. This is a big deal for owners of LT-powered rides that require regular smog testing, and who would like to see a performance increase as well. The 195-cc heads feature their exhaust ports raised .100 inch over stock, but this shouldn't affect header clearances too much. If you've got something that barely

The heads sold by AFR boast full CNC-finishing and outstanding flowbench numbers. They're also priced a bit higher than others on the market, but justify the costs with quality and performance. AFR recently upgraded the entire line of small-block heads, and identify this new generation of heads as "Eliminator" series castings. Pre-Eliminator AFR heads were also very well regarded, but the newest heads have revised port and chamber designs that are even better.

clears now, it might be a concern, but .100 inch isn't much.

The 210-cc AFR head is popular with hotter street machines that aren't smog tested. It's a terrific performer that still uses factory valve spacing, so there aren't any concerns about offset rockers or girdles as with the racier 227-cc head. The 210-cc version flows well enough to feed LT engines pushing more than 400 ci of displacement up to 6,500 rpm (with the proper, matching camshaft) and is ideal for the popular 383- to 396-ci displacements common in these engines when modified for serious street or regular competition use. The exhaust ports are raised .250 inch from the LT1's factory location on this head, which shouldn't be enough to cause any major headaches in most cases, but is something to be aware of. Like all of the AFR heads for LT engines, various combustion chamber sizes are available and all ports/chambers are CNC-finished for the best-possible flow and equality between them.

Dart Machine

Dart offers LT1/LT4 heads in the "Pro1" line. They are top-quality aluminum castings with 58-cc chambers and 2.05-inch intake/1.6-inch exhaust valves. Popular options include intake port sizing (180, 200 or 215 cc), a wide range of valvesprings for various cam designs and profiles, 3/8- or 7/16-inch-diameter rocker arm studs, and stock location ports for compatibility with factory and other aftermarket components. Dart has engineered its LT head design for use with factory-type self-aligning rockers, so pushrod guide plates are not offered.

These budget-friendly heads are also offered bare if you would like to finish them off yourself. They are recommended for stock replacement/upgrade applications and are ideal if you're looking to step up to a higher level of performance without getting too radical. The 58-cc chambers are standard and their design is good for an efficient burn.

Trick Flow Specialties (TFS)

The LT heads from TFS boast larger combustion chamber options (55 or 62 cc), D-shaped exhaust ports (a more efficient design when port sizes are equal), 2.02-inch intake and 1.6-inch exhaust valve diameters, and proprietary "fast-as-cast" 195-cc intake ports. These LT heads are part of TFS's successful Gen-X line of budget-friendly, high-performance castings and are a great choice for a factory replacement head. They are available fully assembled or totally bare, and are designed for no more than .600-inch valve lift as delivered. Naturally, some additional machine work could remedy this, but few LT engines see valve lift beyond .600 anyway.

Brodix

While you may be challenged to find an LT1-specific head on the Brodix website or in the catalog, rest assured Brodix offers LT1 heads. Brodix modifies heads in its Race Rite (RR) series to work on LT engines. Since the modifications are pretty basic, Brodix does the work and sends the heads back in ready-to-install condition.

The Brodix RR are good heads. They're offered in both 180- and 200-cc intake port sizes with 64- or 67-cc combustion chambers, and CNC finishing is available. Additionally, these heads can be had with either straight or angled plugs

Dart's high-quality LT-series castings are based on the highly successful and well-regarded Pro1 products. These heads are budget-friendly as well, and are offered with port finishing at several different sizes (up to 230 cc) to cover the needs of most street and race enthusiasts. Dart also offers a wide range of finishing options, such as various levels of valvesprings, different-diameter rocker studs, etc. Dart also offers the head bare, if you'd like to finish it to your own specifications. This is surely the most laborious option, but also the least expensive way to get a set of brand-new, high-performance heads.

HEADS

Here is the latest and greatest LT-series heads from TFS, featuring the new "fast-as-cast" technology. This means TFS has refined the port designs on both the intake and exhaust sides to flow wonderfully without the need for additional machining.

Trick Flow is constantly refining its products for improved performance and reliability, so if you're looking at some used heads, get as much information as you can about when they were made.

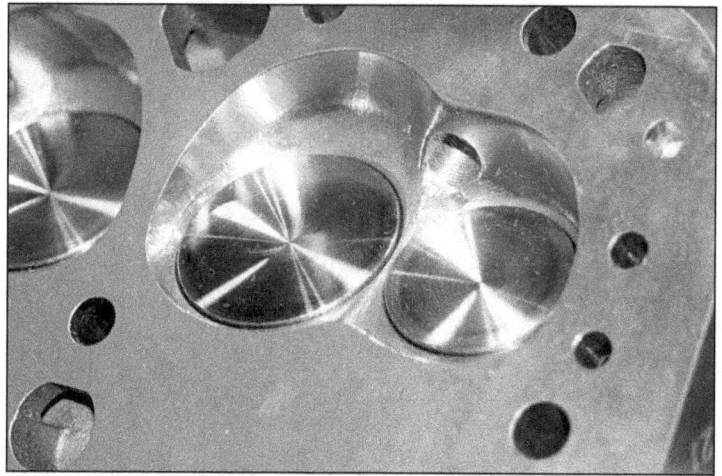

The well-designed combustion chamber encourages unshrouding of the valves and a good, efficient burn. Oversized (compared to factory) valves also allow more volume in and out, which translates to more power.

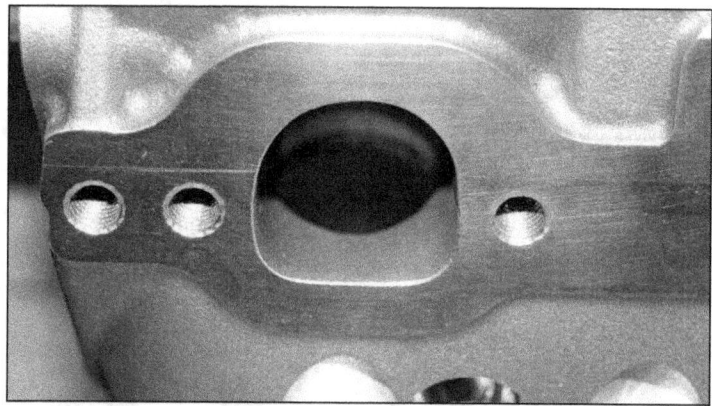

The as-cast finish keeps the incoming fuel in suspension at lower RPM levels (slower airspeeds) and this can be worth power. Hand-ported heads left perfectly smooth have been criticized for this phenomenon. Research has shown the machine finish left by CNC-milling also helps keep fuel in suspension.

CHAPTER 3

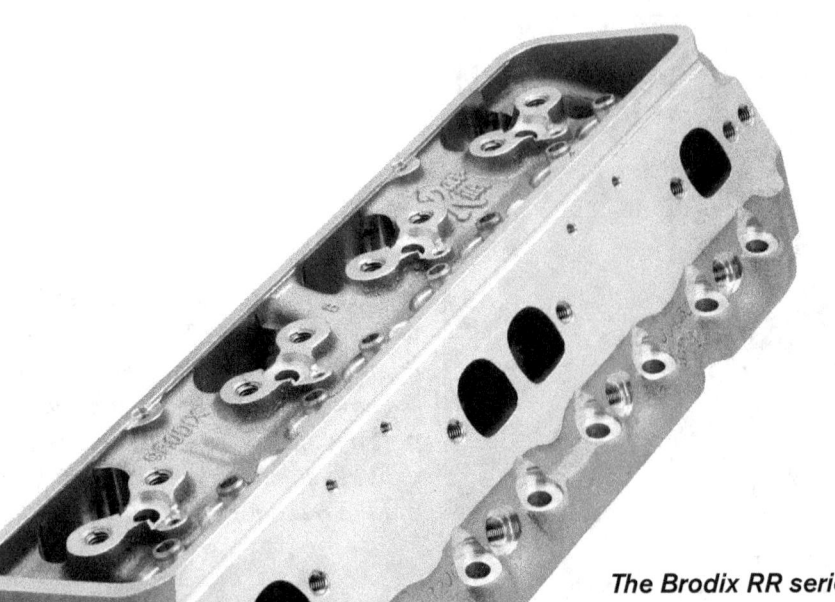

and are ideal for 350- to 406-ci engines. You can get either 2.02 or 2.055-inch-diameter intake valves, and the exhaust valves measure 1.6 inches in diameter. The Brodix RR heads bolt right up where the factory heads were, and the exhaust ports are in the stock location as well.

The Brodix RR series of small-block heads have gained favor with enthusiasts due to their performance-per-dollar value and top quality. Brodix offers the RR line to LT1 enthusiasts as converted small-block heads (as opposed to a dedicated LT casting). This is a perfectly acceptable option and you should keep it in mind when shopping for heads. Unlike other small-block heads, Brodix doesn't charge extra for the conversion at this time. If you purchase used or non-LT heads and have them converted by a capable engine shop, there is additional labor costs involved. If you have Brodix do the work, the quality is top-notch and there's no additional fee. That's something to remember.

Air Flow Research Heads

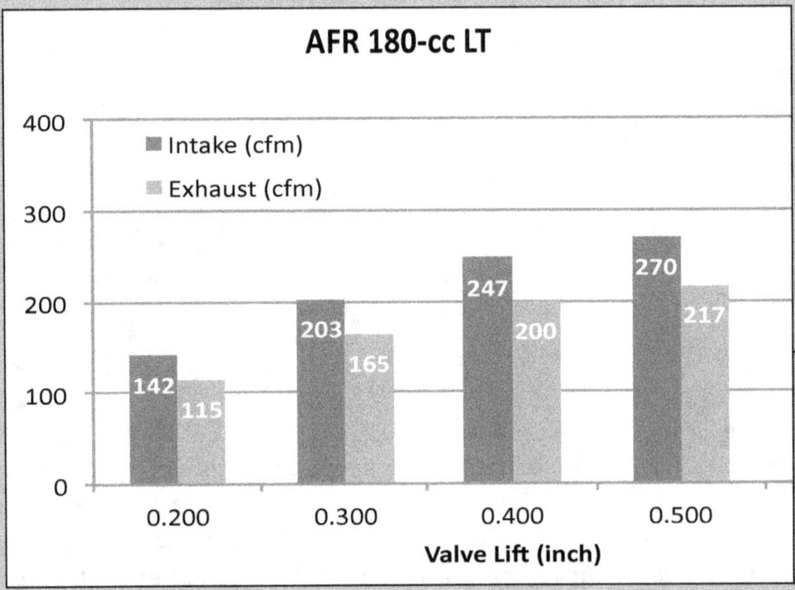

AFR 180-cc LT

Valve Lift (inch)	Intake (cfm)	Exhaust (cfm)
0.200	142	115
0.300	203	165
0.400	247	200
0.500	270	217

HEADS

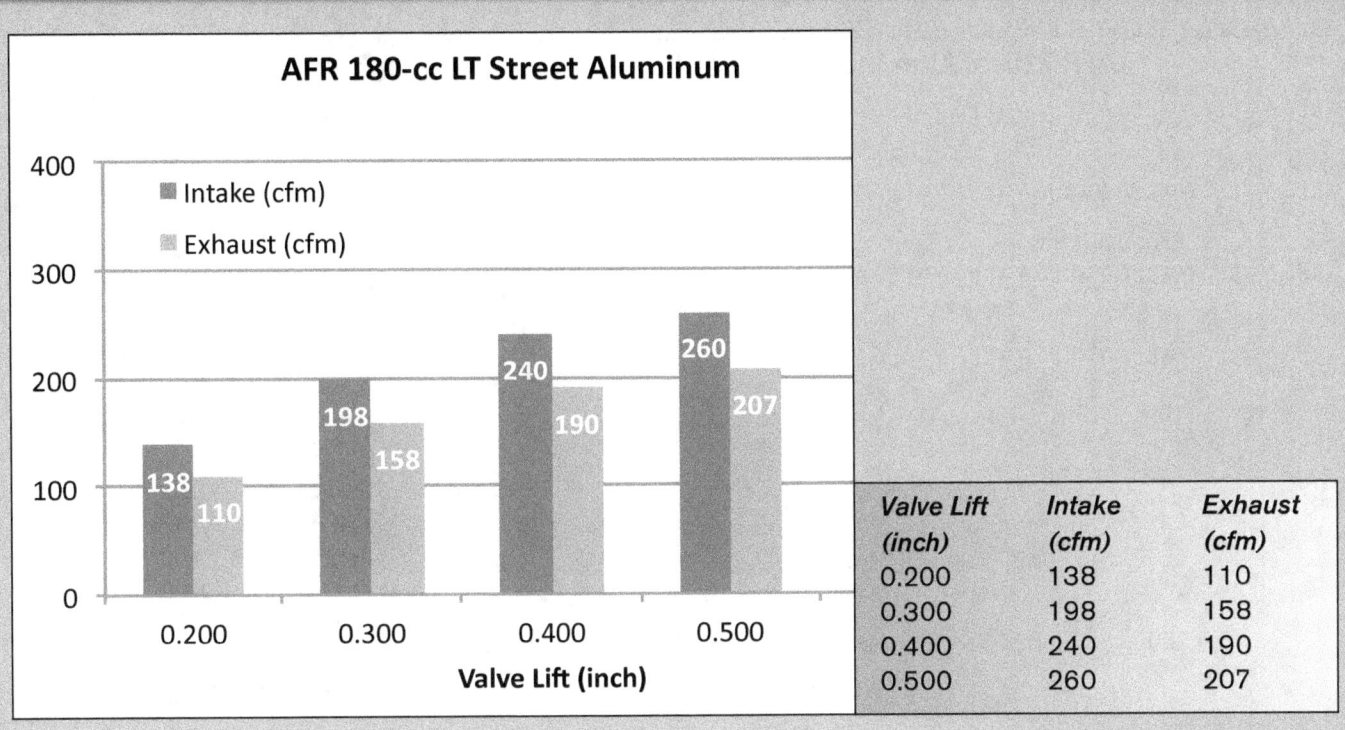

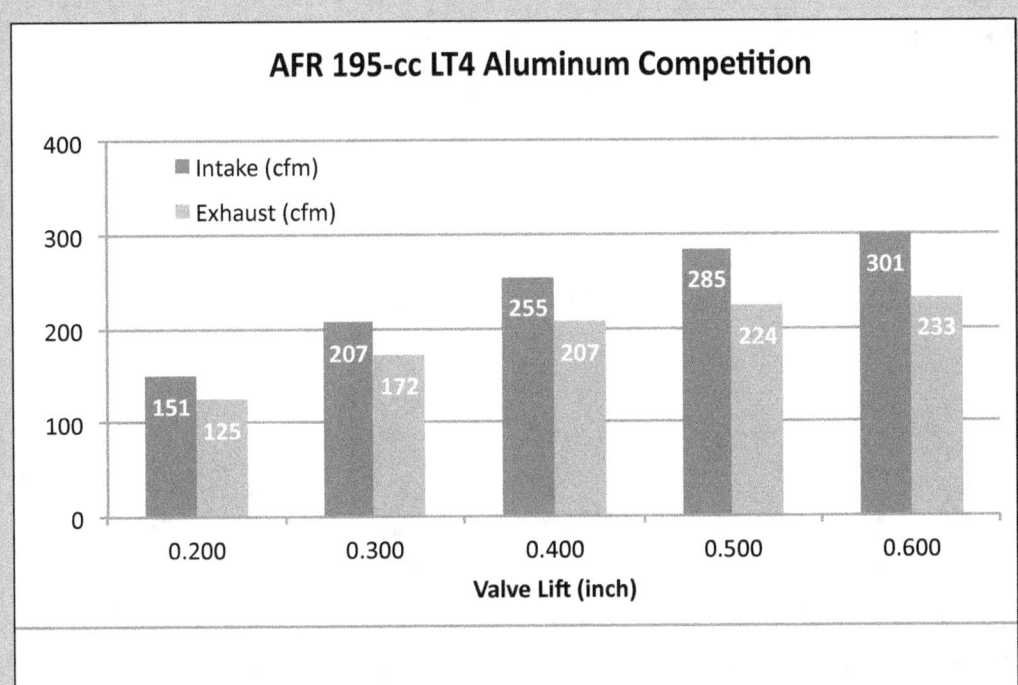

Air Flow Research Heads *CONTINUED*

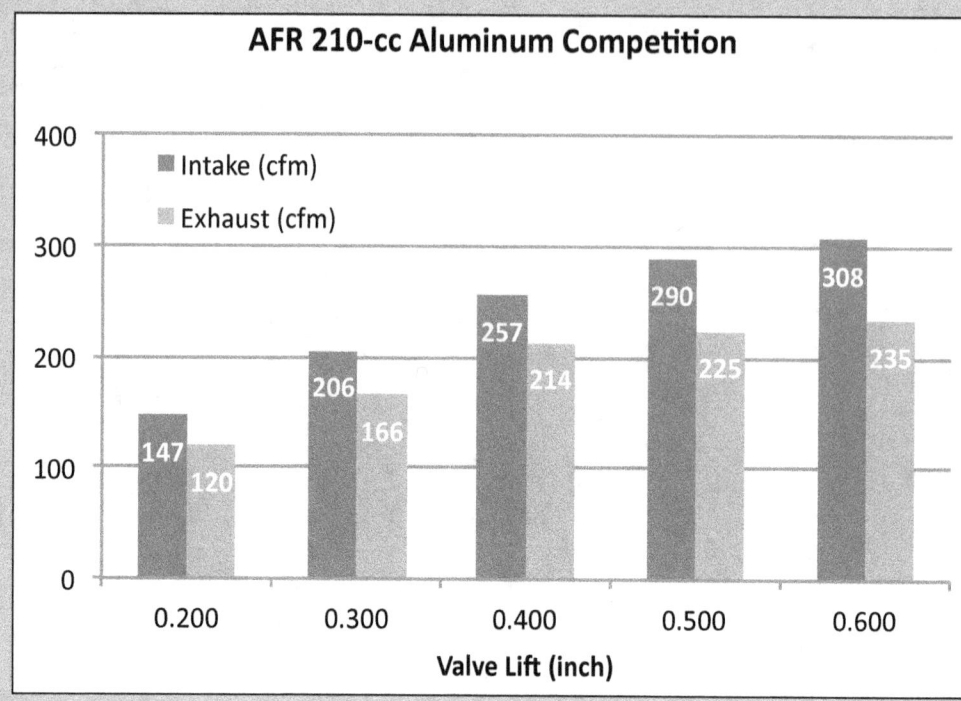

AFR 210-cc Aluminum Competition

Valve Lift (inch)	Intake (cfm)	Exhaust (cfm)
0.200	147	120
0.300	206	166
0.400	257	214
0.500	290	225
0.600	308	235

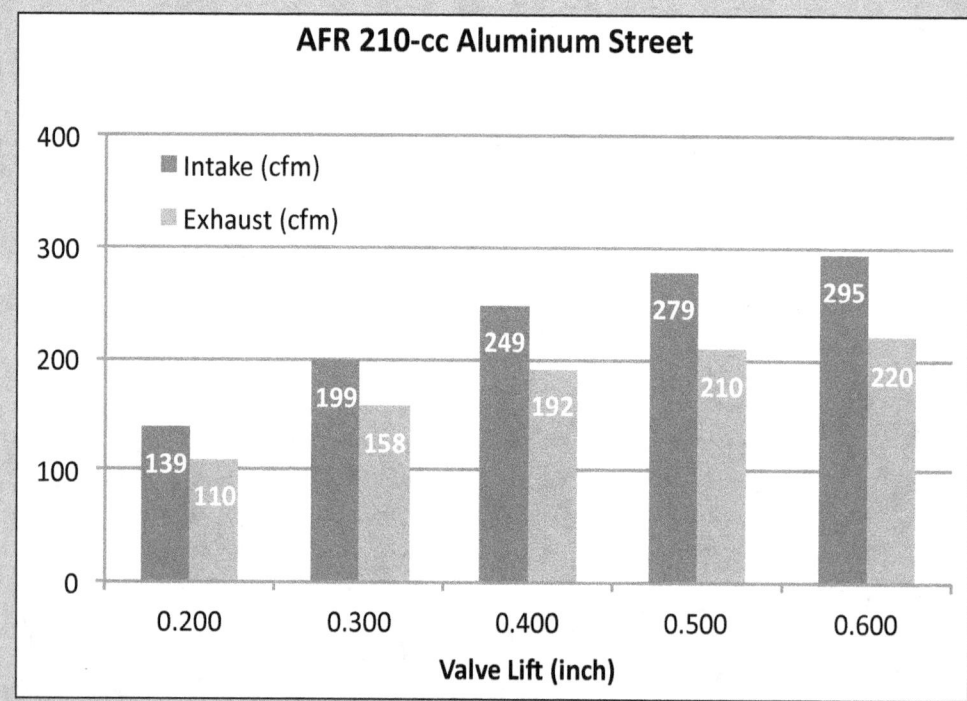

AFR 210-cc Aluminum Street

Valve Lift (inch)	Intake (cfm)	Exhaust (cfm)
0.200	139	110
0.300	199	158
0.400	249	192
0.500	279	210
0.600	295	220

HEADS

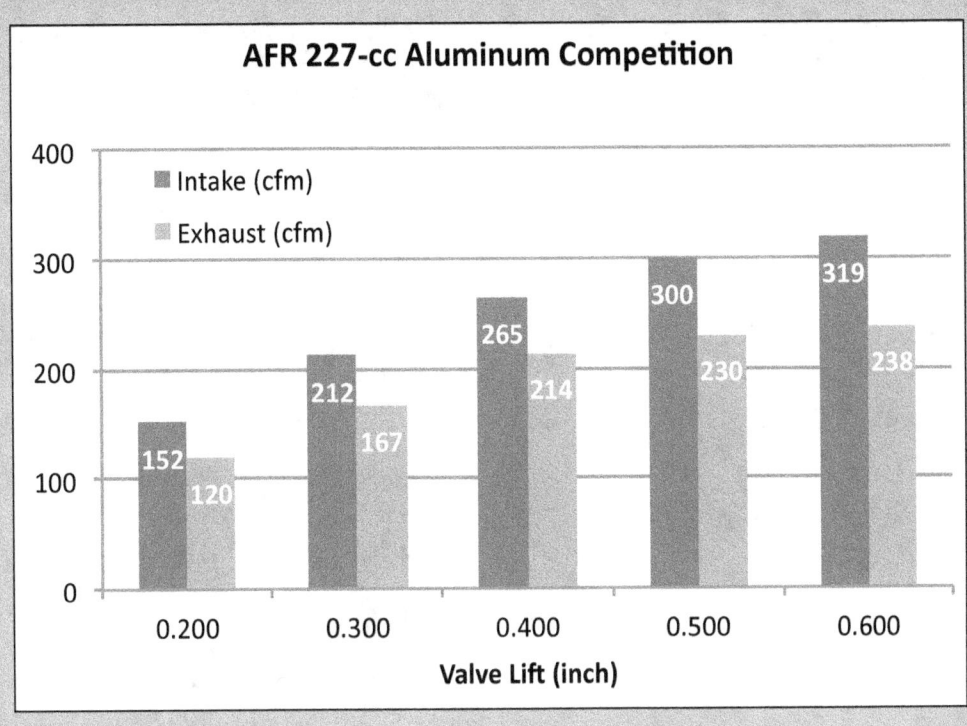

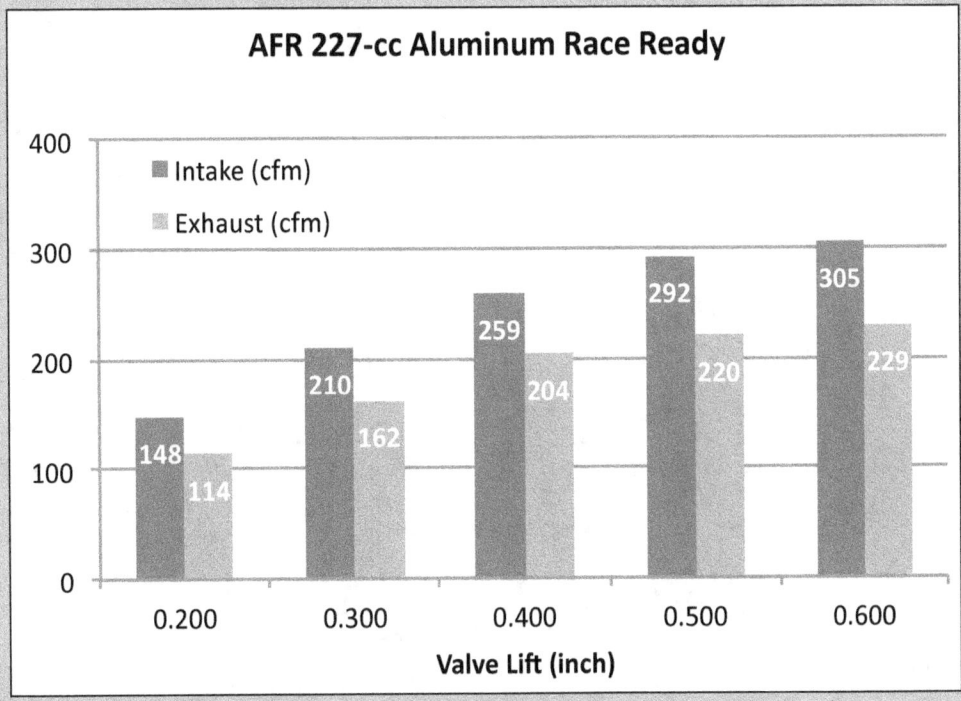

CHAPTER 3

Dart Machine Heads

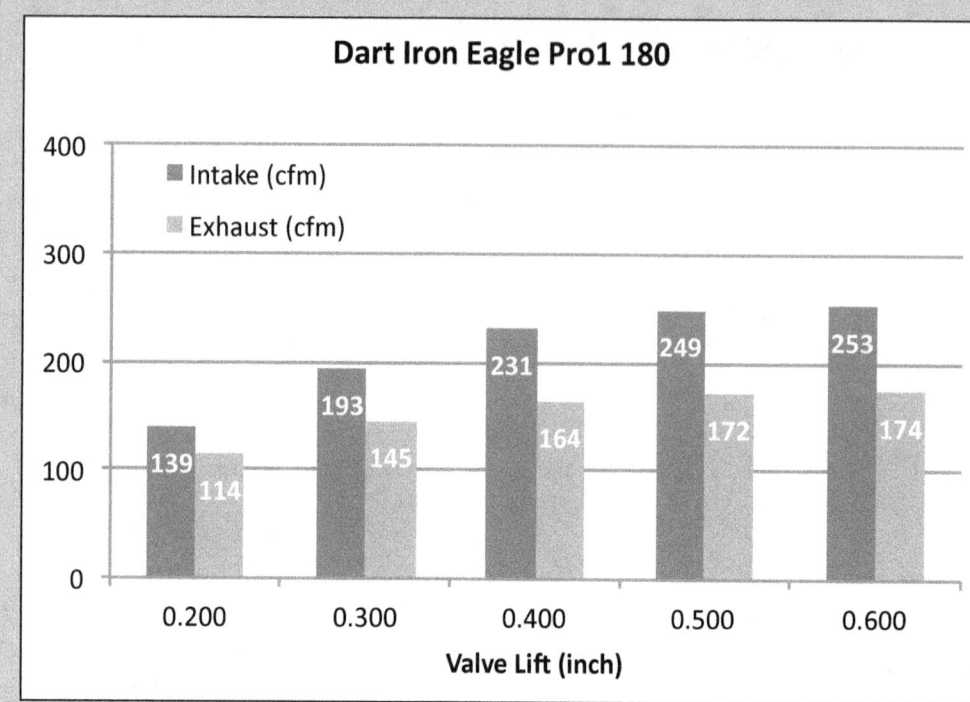

Valve Lift (inch)	Intake (cfm)	Exhaust (cfm)
0.200	139	114
0.300	193	145
0.400	231	164
0.500	249	172
0.600	253	174

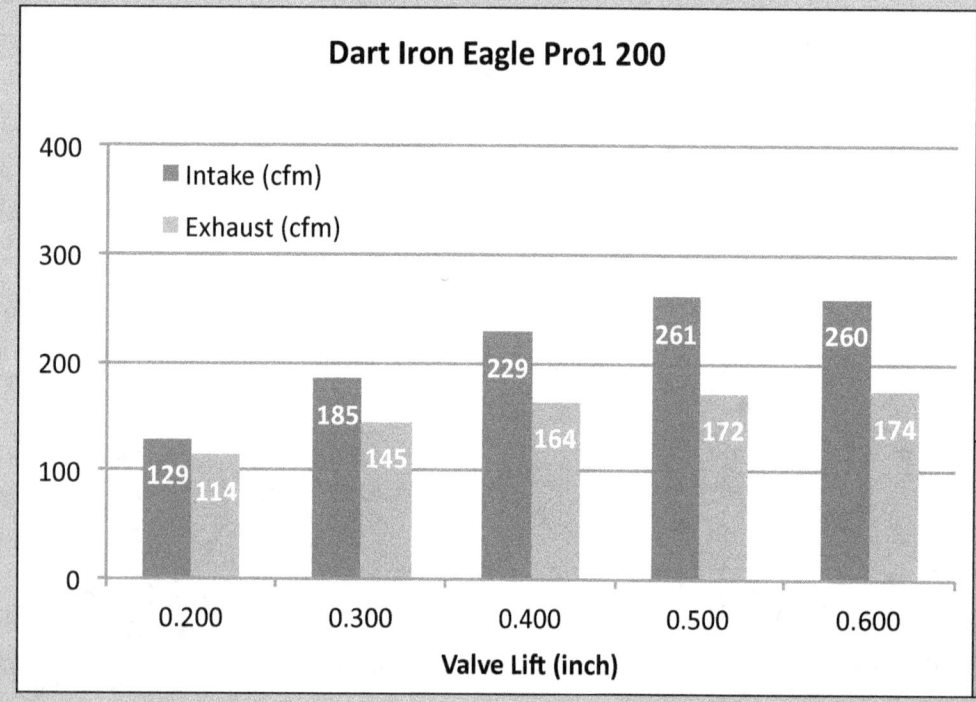

Valve Lift (inch)	Intake (cfm)	Exhaust (cfm)
0.200	129	114
0.300	185	145
0.400	229	164
0.500	261	172
0.600	260	174

HEADS

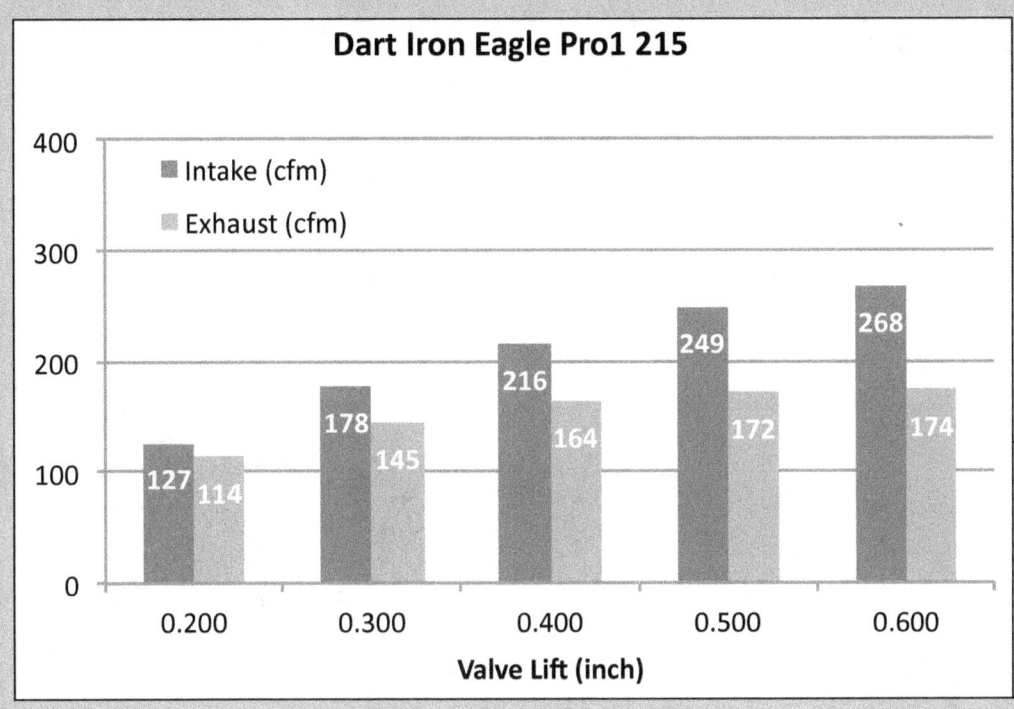

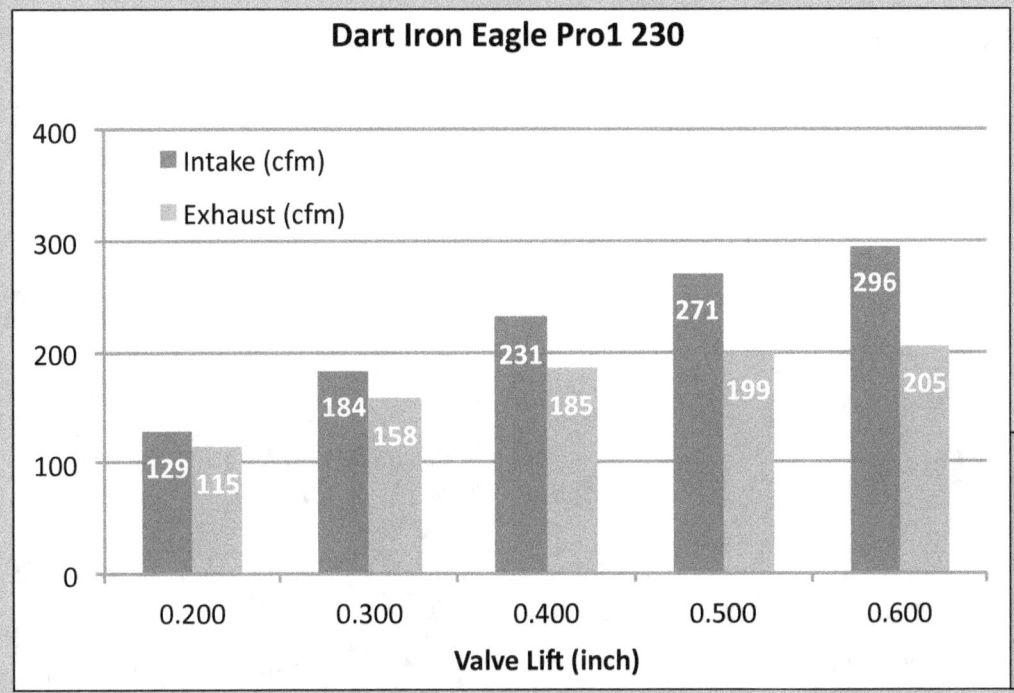

Trick Flow Specialties Heads

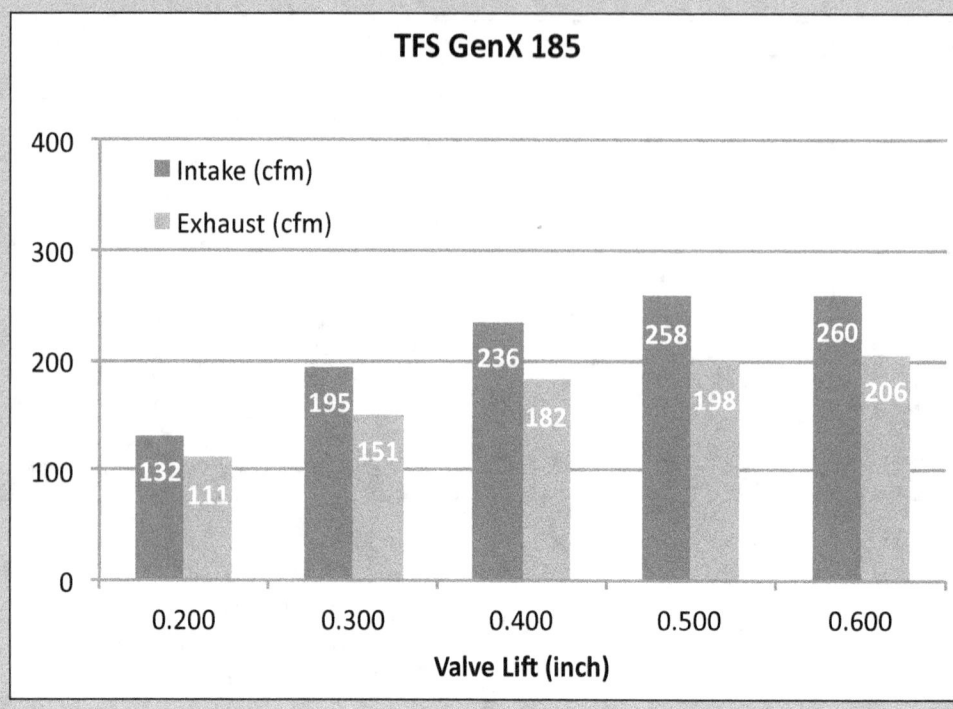

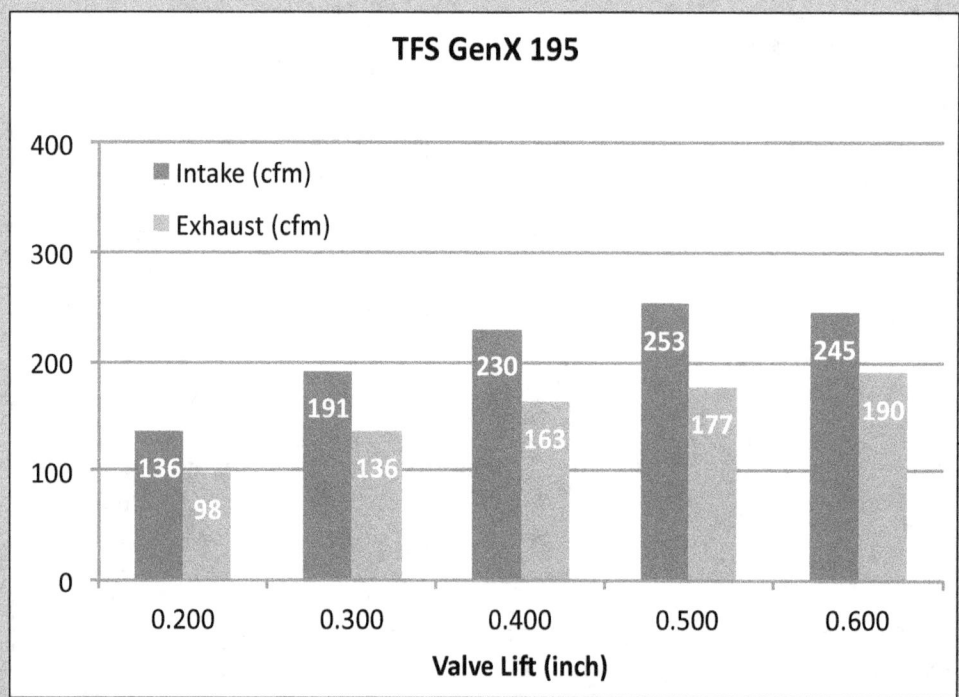

HEADS

Brodix Heads

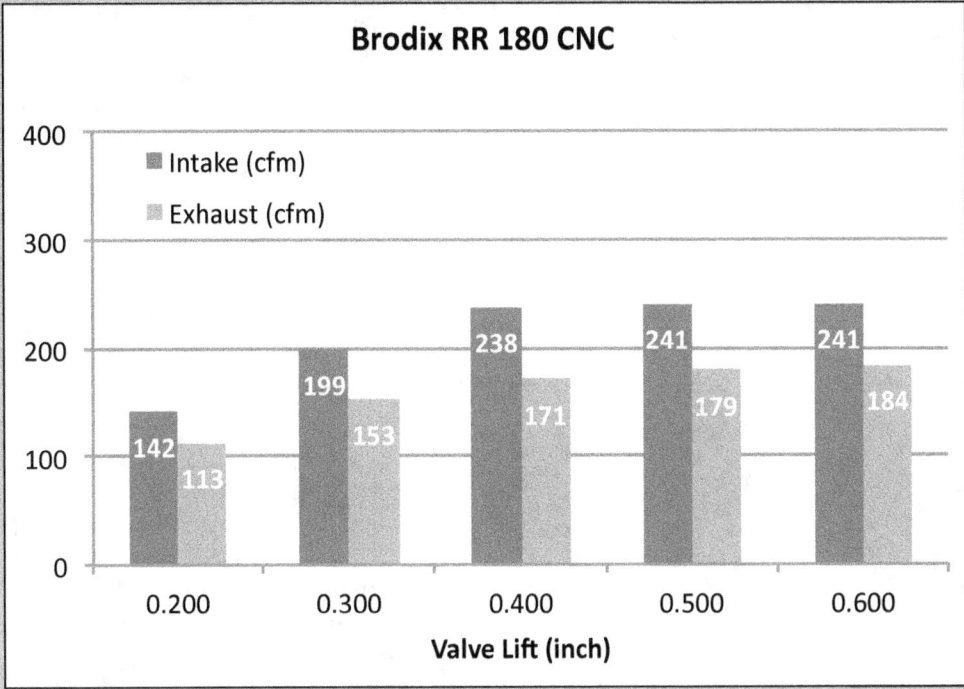

Valve Lift (inch)	Intake (cfm)	Exhaust (cfm)
0.200	142	113
0.300	199	153
0.400	238	171
0.500	241	179
0.600	241	184

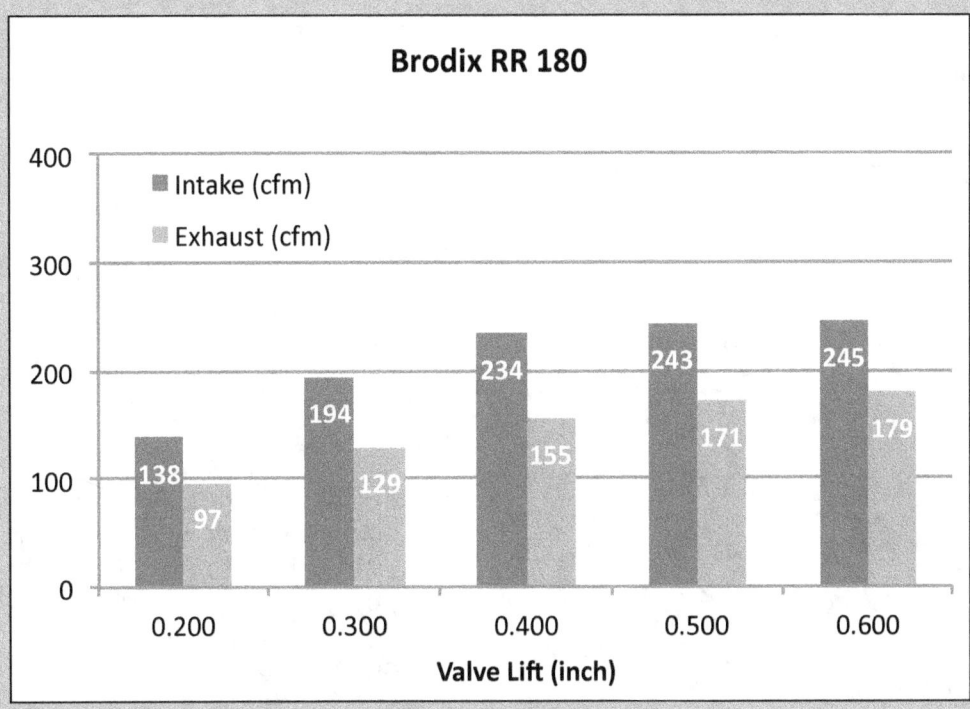

Valve Lift (inch)	Intake (cfm)	Exhaust (cfm)
0.200	138	97
0.300	194	129
0.400	234	155
0.500	243	171
0.600	245	179

Brodix Heads CONTINUED

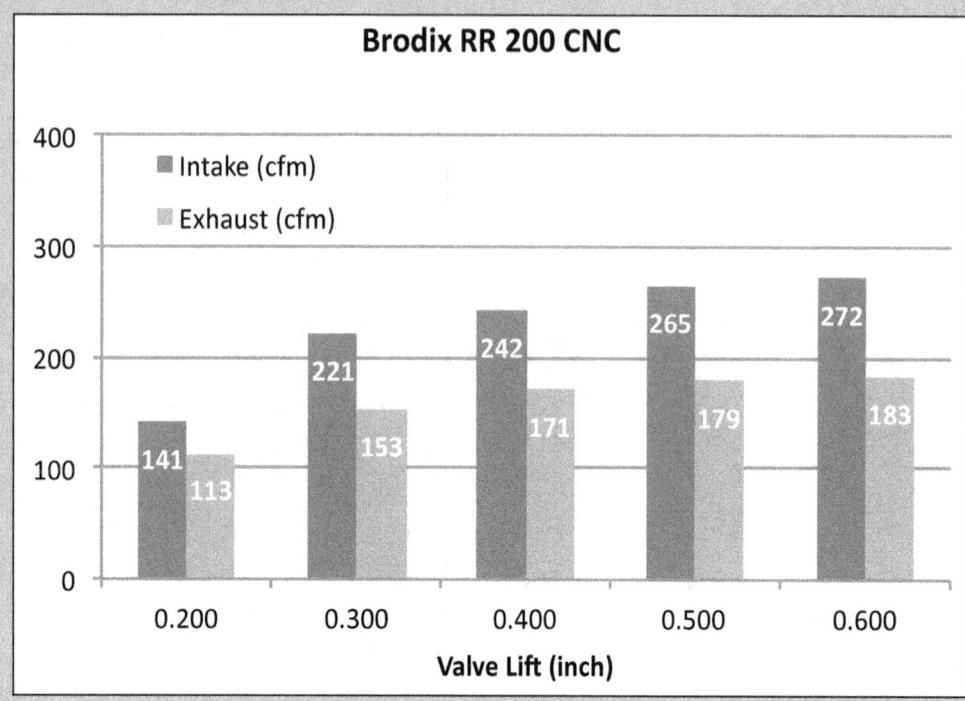

Valve Lift (inch)	Intake (cfm)	Exhaust (cfm)
0.200	141	113
0.300	221	153
0.400	242	171
0.500	265	179
0.600	272	183

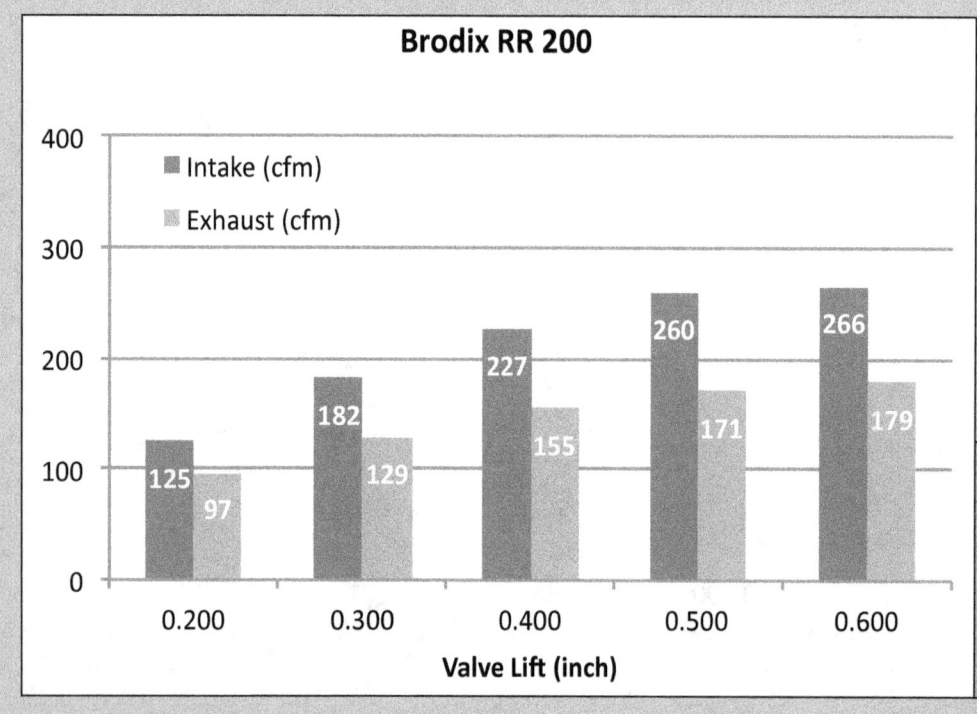

Valve Lift (inch)	Intake (cfm)	Exhaust (cfm)
0.200	125	97
0.300	182	129
0.400	227	155
0.500	260	171
0.600	266	179

CHAPTER 4

VALVETRAIN

The LT1/LT4 camshaft, lifter tappet, pushrod, and rocker design are typical for American V-8s in general and small-block Chevrolet engines in particular. There is nothing distinctive or unique about the design or the individual components.

The two main visual differences between the LT1 and the LT4 are the rocker arms (which are aluminum and are of a roller-tip design) and the color of the intake (which is red for the LT4). The easiest way to tell you have the important parts is to remove a valve cover and inspect the rocker arms. If yours has an aluminum rocker set, it is most likely an LT4. At this point, it might be wise to also check the cylinder head casting number, which is visible with the valve cover removed.

The LT4s hollow-stemmed valves are of lighter weight (see Chapter 3) and this has an impact on your valvetrain choice. These small variations (aluminum roller rockers and hollow-stemmed valves) allow the LT4 to have an elevated 6,400-rpm capability (versus 5,700 rpm for the LT1). The better-quality LT4 components are worth keeping if you have them, but comparable parts are available in the aftermarket to upgrade LT1s as well.

Timing Chain and Cover

There are three different front covers for the timing chain. From 1992 to 1994, the timing chain cover had a small hole for the distributor drive. From 1994 to 1995 it has a larger hole for the distributor drive. From 1996 to 1997 it has the larger hole for the distributor as well as a provision for the crank position sensor to accommodate the OBDII engine management system.

The front of the cylinder block is the same from 1992 to 1997, which means you can use whichever cam, timing chain cover, and distributor you choose as long as they are from the corresponding year and are a matching set.

There are three variations of the timing chain set for the LT engine. The early style is unique because it employs a small driveshaft between the distributor and the cam gear. This setup makes it very difficult to index the distributor rotor correctly. Be patient and make sure you install it with a light touch; do not force these components together during assembly, as damage is likely to occur.

The second timing chain design made installation much simpler, since it has only one long pin that drives it, versus the splined driveshaft used in the earlier version. The second design has almost the same durability as the first, but is still less desirable than the third iteration.

Stock oil pump gear. Notice the single line on the gear. This is a stock LT gear that is compatible with cams with heat-treated gears.

CHAPTER 4

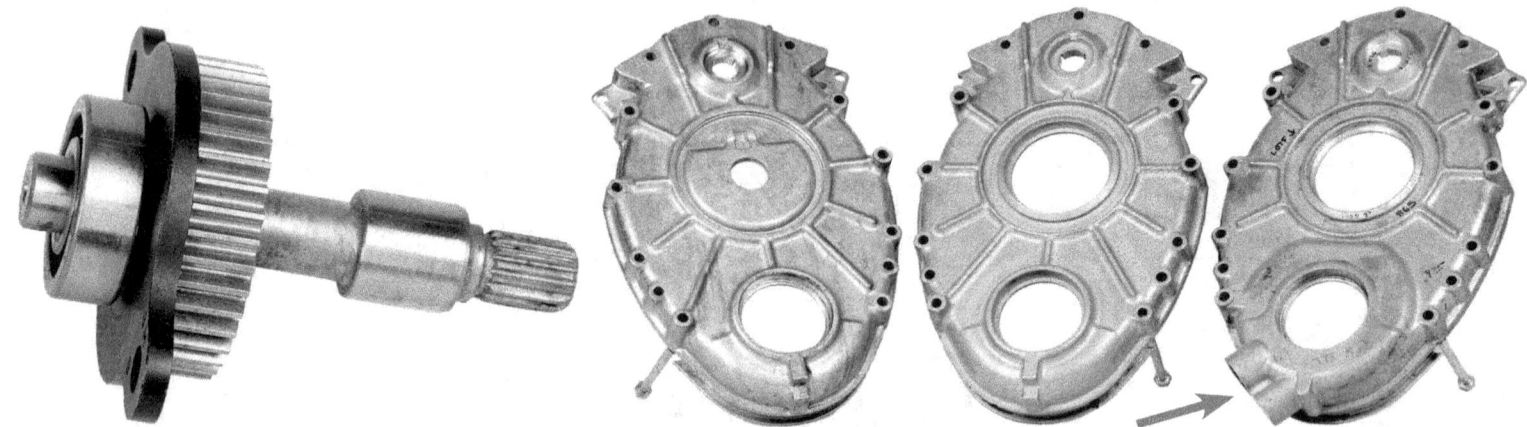

Stock water pump drive. No aftermarket replacement parts available.

Left: early-style 1992 and 1993 timing set cover; middle: 1994 and 1995 cover; right: 1996 and 1997 timing set cover. Notice the crank sensor mount (arrow) on the late style.

The first production LT1 chain was a "link"-style chain. The second design turned into a "bicycle" style. The LT4 version is much more of a true roller style.

Camshaft

All of the factory-design camshafts for the LT1/LT4 engines are of the hydraulic roller variety. Generally speaking, there are five different camshaft grinds.

The camshafts for all LT1 and LT4 engines are the same; the only difference is the length of the drive pin and the center hole to receive a late-model distributor.

There are two styles of camshaft snout. The "early" snout from 1992 to 1995 with aluminum heads has a shallow hole and a short drive pin. The "late" snout from 1995 to 1997 with aluminum heads has a larger, deeper hole and a longer drive pin. Any GM small-block camshaft can be drilled for the late-design distributor to install the long pin. All iron-headed LT1s have the late-style cam snout.

When measuring your camshaft, make sure your test data is collected at the same value. The industry standard is .050-inch lift, and you see cam specifications called out at this lift dimension on cam cards and spec sheets.

These factory camshafts do not have casting numbers like most other parts of the engine. Instead they are stamped with ID numbers.

Lifters

The factory lifters in the LT engines are all of the same design: hydraulic rollers. These are interchangeable with all hydraulic-roller, small-block Chevrolet engines dating back to the late-1986 Corvette. All aluminum-headed engines (including the L98 and LT1/LT4) can accept this style of lifter without modification.

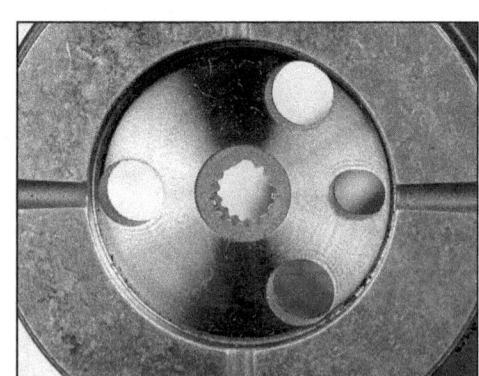

Left: early-style LT timing chain gear with a splined distributor drive center hole; right: late-style gear with smooth hole; pin driven.

HOW TO BUILD MAX-PERFORMANCE CHEVY LT1/LT4 ENGINES

VALVETRAIN

A completed and installed cam and timing set.

Here we point out the only way a cam can be installed on the timing set, making it virtually idiot proof.

Left: standard LT timing chain and gear; right: LT4 gear and chain.

Left: late stock LT1 chain and gear; middle: stock LT4 chain and gear; right: aftermarket billet gear and true roller chain. Notice the bulk of the chain and gear set.

Note the larger center hole in the longer-drive-pin version.

Long versus short drive pin.

Cam ID Numbers

ID Number	Engine
241	1992–1995 350 with aluminum heads (Note .450-inch-diameter hole in cam nose with .322-inch dowel pin for cam gear)
600 or 779	1994–1996 350 with iron heads (.500 x 1.062-inch center hole and .246-inch dowel pin)
705 or 242	1996–1997 350 with aluminum heads (.500 x 1.062-inch center hole and .246-inch dowel pin)
12551705	1995–1997 Reference number (Corvette/Camaro)
12551142	1996 LT4 Reference number (Corvette)

Cam Grinds

While there have been many variations of the camshafts, they are not all equal. Fairly common grinds are:

705 (LT1)
Duration .050
Intake 203 degrees
Exhaust 208 degrees
Lift
  .450 inch intake
  .460 inch exhaust
Lobe Separation Angle
  114 degrees

242 (LT4)
Duration .050
Intake 203 degrees
Exhaust 210 degrees
Lift
  .476 inch intake
  .480 inch exhaust
Lobe Separation Angle
  115 degrees

The factory tie bars are a simple and effective design. Once secured by the steel "spider" retainer, they can be trusted to maintain lifter alignment to the cam lobe.

Common LT1/LT4 Camshafts

The following a list of the aftermarket TPIS camshafts most commonly used in high-performance LT1/LT4 engines. These cams have all been developed over time, tested rigorously, and proven to work effectively in the applications they're intended for.

Super Profile L98

This is a camshaft that we used in the SCCA World Challenge when we had to run a stock camshaft. This cam passes tech for lift and seat duration. There is more area under the curve. This cam has a very aggressive acceleration rate of the valve off the seat, yet it is not so harsh that it kills springs and pushrods.

Duration at .050: 220/220
Lift: .420/.420
Lobe Separation Angle: 112 degrees

With this cam you can barely hear that anything has been done; very smooth idle. The dyno gains over the stock cam were on the order of 30 ft-lbs and 20 hp. Engines equipped with this cam easily rev to 5,800 rpm. A great first step for a street engine.

ZZ-9

This camshaft was developed for our 1994 emissions-legal Camaro that was featured in the June 1995 issue of *Car Craft* magazine. The cam is emissions legal when used in our 400-hp kit. It has a noticeable lope at idle. On the lopey idle scale of 1 to 10, the ZZ-9 is a 3.

Duration at .050: 212/226
Lift: .483/.520
Lobe Separation Angle: 112 degrees
This cam needs computer programming to get the idle stabilized. Its redline is about 6,200 rpm.

ZZ-9X

This is a very nice set of lobes, but to run it you need to upgrade the valvesprings.

Duration at .050: 226/239
Lift: .520/.558
Lobe Separation Angle: 112 degrees

This cam's redline is at 6,500 rpm. On a scale of 1 to 10, the lopey idle value is about 4. If you select this cam, you need to get your computer reprogrammed. It won't idle properly or run correctly with the factory computer tuning once this camshaft is in place.

ZZ-10

This cam is for the "bigger is better" crowd.

Duration at .050: 233/240
Lift: .538/.560
Lobe Separation Angle: 112 degrees

On a scale of 1 to 10, this cam has a lopey idle value of 5. It's very noticeable and now you're in a range of cams where custom computer programming is needed. This cam needs a higher compression ratio, improved intake and exhaust systems, and near 7,000 rpm to really show what it can do.

ZZ-409

If your engine plans include a stroke for greater displacement, the ZZ-409 with its single-pattern profile is a good call. It's got a noticeable idle (lopey cam score of 4) and, of course, it requires reprogramming of the ECU, but it makes great power in big-inch LT1/LT4 engines.

Duration at .050: 226/226
Lift: .520/.520
Lobe Separation Angle: 112 degrees

ZZ-X

This is a pretty serious cam for hot street cars or competition machines that see 7,000 rpm. It needs at least 11:1 compression, good headers, and a high-flow intake system with a larger-than-stock throttle body. Its rough-idle characteristics give it an 8 on the lopey cam scale, and it probably needs to idle at 1,000 rpm out of gear. If you want to make some serious power at high RPM, this cam delivers.

CHAPTER 4

Common LT1/LT4 Camshafts CONTINUED

Duration at .050: 239/239
Lift: .558/.558
Lobe Separation Angle: 112 degrees

Of course, any combination of lobes can be ground to suit any particular application. Solid-roller lobes are a little harsher than those of a hydraulic roller.

One secret to making power is how fast you can open the intake valve the first .100 inch. If it's too aggressive, you end up with broken parts. Cam manufacturers use terms like "high energy" or "high intensity" to describe this phenomenon.

Just a note about running serious cams like these: Steel or stainless-steel full-roller rocker arms make more horsepower throughout the RPM range than aluminum roller rockers. A steel rocker arm is simply more rigid than an aluminum example. Therefore, more energy is transmitted to the valve when a steel arm is used.

The weight of the components on the pushrod side of the rocker stud is not nearly as important as the weight on the valve side. Hollow-stem valves (such as those found on the LT4 heads) and lightweight retainers are a tremendous aid to valvetrain stability at higher (6,000-plus) RPM.

Tie Bars

These pieces slip over the lifters to help maintain accurate alignment between the lobe on the camshaft and the wheel on the lifter. There are no differences between versions of the LT engine for this component of the engine.

Spider Spring

This piece bolts to the lifter valley to hold the tie bars in place. There are three bosses that allow you to attach the spider spring to the valley. Once again, these are all interchangeable on all factory-installed roller lifter small-block Chevrolet engines.

Pushrods

The pushrods for all LT engines are interchangeable and no differences can be found between LT1 and LT4 variations.

Rocker Arms

All LT1/LT4 Engines have self-aligning rocker arms. This is accomplished with a shoulder at the valve end of the rocker arm, which cradles the tip of the valvestem. The LT1 has the traditional stamped-steel rocker arm and ball pivot with a friction lock nut; these are a nominal 1.5:1. The LT 4 has aluminum rocker arms featuring a roller bearing on the pivot as well as on the tip. These have a 1.6:1 ratio, and are adjusted by a posi-lock nut design.

Rocker Studs

The stud in the head holds the rocker arm in place and allows it to pivot. These are all the same across the line-up for small-block Chevrolet engines with aluminum heads. They are a screw-in type and are 3/8 inch in diameter on the top and have 7/16-inch threads on the bottom. This style and size is fairly typical for most Chevrolet engines. They can be easily upgraded to stronger 7/16-inch studs, and the added strength contributes to a crisper valve opening and greater valvetrain durability.

Valve Locks and Retainers

The retainers on the LT1 are stamped steel, as are those found on the LT4. The slight difference between the two is that the LT4 retainers are slightly lighter.

Spring Seats

All aluminum heads need a steel spring seat cup to prevent erosion of the head.

Valves and Valvesprings

All LT-series V-8s share the same factory valvespring.

CHAPTER 5

AIR AND FUEL MANAGEMENT

The differences in air and fuel management between the LT1 and LT4 engines are relatively minor. The major components of this aspect of the engine are the intake casting and the cylinder head casting. This chapter covers the different sensors required to keep the engine alive and some minor changes in the development of the LT series.

Intakes: LT1 vs. LT4

The main engineering difference between the LT1 and LT4 intake manifolds are that metal was added to the top of the gasket surface of the LT4 intake because the LT4 cylinder heads have a raised intake port location. But, in raising the port, the factory did not enlarge the LT4 port; the location was simply changed its location. Because of this, the ports do not flow as well as the original LT1 version.

As mentioned, metal was added to the LT4 intake manifold to ensure proper gasket sealing. General Motors did not change the shape of the port interior; it changed the shape of the mounting flange where it mounts to the head.

After many airflow tests, we have noticed no discernable difference between the LT1 and LT4 intake manifolds. The performance of the two are exactly identical, given they are mounted to the exact same cylinder head configuration.

The bolt patterns on the LT1 and LT4 intakes are vastly changed from the previous Gen I (1955-up 265- to 400-ci) small-block. It goes without saying that early-style intake manifolds simply do not fit on Gen II LT-series heads. Both LT1 and LT4 intakes feature a one-piece cast-aluminum design with no coolant crossover passages.

Several intakes are available to help you swap out the fuel injection for a 4-barrel conversion. Once

Typical LT4 red-painted intake. Don't be fooled by the fancy paint, this does not flow any better than the stock LT1 intake.

CHAPTER 5

Hunting Horsepower

The following is an airflow study that was done while developing a line of products for the C4 Corvette. The information is also relevant to vehicles that were equipped with LT1/LT4 engines from the factory.

For years, the standard test pressure for 4-barrel carburetors has been 20.4 inches of water. This is the vacuum level used under the carb when it is rated. By establishing a standard, various types of carburetor could be tested side-by-side. When you see a carb rated at 750 cfm, for example, that means it is capable of flowing 750 cubic feet of air per minute when there are 20.4 inches of vacuum under it.

The standard for cylinder head flow bench work has been slowly creeping upward for years. For a while it was 25 inches, and then as engine builders got better equipment, it changed to 28 inches. Some of our early cylinder head studies were done at 25, and recent tests are done at 28. (In all cases, the test pressures are listed.)

The numbers you see here all represent dry flow. If this were a carburetor, fuel would also be present (called wet flow) and would reduce the air numbers by about 10 percent, since liquid would restrict the flow of air. So, a carburetor would have to flow about 750 cfm to have the same airflow capacity as a dry throttle body that dry flows 668 cfm of air alone.

This series of 11 tests is on the area of filter lid to throttle body (using the Corvette system): air filter lid, actual air filter element, air filter body, Mass Air Flow Sensor (MAF), rubber bellows, and throttle body. All data is corrected to 20.4 inches of water, which is the rating for a Holley 4-barrel carburetor.

Test 1 (see Chart A)

This test was performed with a stock filter and lid, MAF with screens, and stock throttle body.

Test 2 (see Chart A)

We removed the screens, which is a typical first modification. Notice that this produces the biggest single gain (78 cfm). This is something you can do yourself.

Test 2a (see Chart A)

We then installed the TPIS Airfoil so we could see what it would do at this point.

Test 3 (see Chart A)

We installed the TPIS Air Filter for a 17-cfm gain (the Airfoil was removed).

Test 4 (see Chart A)

In this test we cut the air filter lid to increase the airflow. Again we saw a nice gain (26 cfm). This is one of those jobs you can do yourself and save the money a shop would charge to do it for you.

Test 5 (see Charts A)

When we modified the MAF sensor, we reshaped the inside surface. It still appeared stock on the outside. A modified MAF sensor provided a small, but solid gain of 14 cfm. This is also one of those jobs you could do yourself and save the money a shop would charge for the labor.

Test 6 (see Chart A)

This test shows the TPIS Airfoil installed. You might ask, "Okay, where's the 40 cfm I've seen advertised?" Well, you're right, it only gains 16 cfm when installed in the whole system. You need to look at tests 7 through 11, (Charts D and E) to get the full picture.

Test 7 (see Chart B)

Here we test the throttle body all by itself; 668 cfm.

Test 8 (see Chart B)

This test shows a 41-cfm gain. It is the same as Test 7 except that the TPIS Airfoil has been installed. Now you see the 40-plus-cfm promised. If you take the 709 and add 10 percent because it remains dry, you end up with 779 cfm. This should pass enough air to make 400-plus-hp if everything else is up to snuff.

We have tested the oval-bore (one-blade) throttle bodies on a 406-ci engine which produced 510 ft-lbs of torque and 446 hp with a stock throttle body and TPIS Airfoil. We found no power gains at all. However, this type of throttle body may offer a power increase when installed on a system that has a higher airflow capacity than a TPI system. TPIS has a new Mini-Ram intake manifold that uses a single butterfly throttle body to some advantage.

AIR AND FUEL MANAGEMENT

We have also adapted GM electronics to Edelbrock and Weiand single-plane manifolds. In some of these installations, the stock throttle body appears to be restricting the system, so a single butterfly throttle body may be of some advantage. As it currently stands, a stock throttle body with a TPIS Airfoil is the most efficient and cost effective means of optimizing the flow of a TPI system.

Test 9 (see Chart C)
Here, we look at the MAF sensor, 529-cfm stock.

Test 10 (see Chart C)
When we remove both screens, we see a 182-cfm gain! If you've been keeping track, you may be thinking this isn't making complete sense. Well, you're right. The one thing that wasn't tested by itself yet was the air filter body. We know that the final number in Test 6 was 585 cfm, and yet the MAF in Test 11 is 750 cfm and the throttle body alone with TPIS Airfoil in place is 709 cfm. We can probably deduce that the filter assembly on a Corvette cost about 65 cfm.

Now the question is, Is it the filter or the body? The filter body, in this case, happened to be one of the worst ones we had to test at the time. The body is worth about 60 cfm and the filter, about 5 cfm. (See Chart D for the real story on filter housings). Because of the restrictions of the stock housing, the performance aftermarket now offers high-flow versions.

Test 11 (see Chart C)
Here we tested with screens removed and internal surfaces smoothed.

TPIS is the inventor and patent holder of the Airfoil. As with any good idea, there will always be less inventive souls who will copy it. There is another Airfoil on the market that is basically held in by the ducting. Our research showed this type of mount is simply not good enough. In our testing, the duct-mounted Airfoil showed no airflow improvement on the flow bench, and we actually had trouble keeping it mounted in place on the dyno.

If you compare Chart E to Chart F, you see the total gains in airflow that are possible. The engine shown in Chart F has siamesed intake tubes and the following TPIS parts: ported and polished cylinder heads, max-ported base, ported plenum, Airfoil, fuel-pressure regulator, roller rockers, spark-plug wires, camshaft, and modified mass airflow sensor.

We wanted to see what the Airfoil would do on a stock engine with the screens removed. Chart E is an engine dyno test on a 1985 Corvette 350 that has 50,000 street miles and 6,000 racing miles plus more than 500 dyno runs. Everything is stock except for dyno headers. For this test the screens have be removed, as this is the first thing most people do.

Using a TPIS-modified MAF as the control orifice, we picked five stock Corvette filter housings at random and tested them. The difference is a whopping 88 cfm! Now you can begin to see why some cars are faster than

This is an early-style factory throttle body shown next to an identical one that has been bored out to 52 mm from the stock 48 mm, and a throttle body airfoil has been added. This style of throttle body has an adjustable TPS, which is set to .54 volt.

Hunting Horsepower CONTINUED

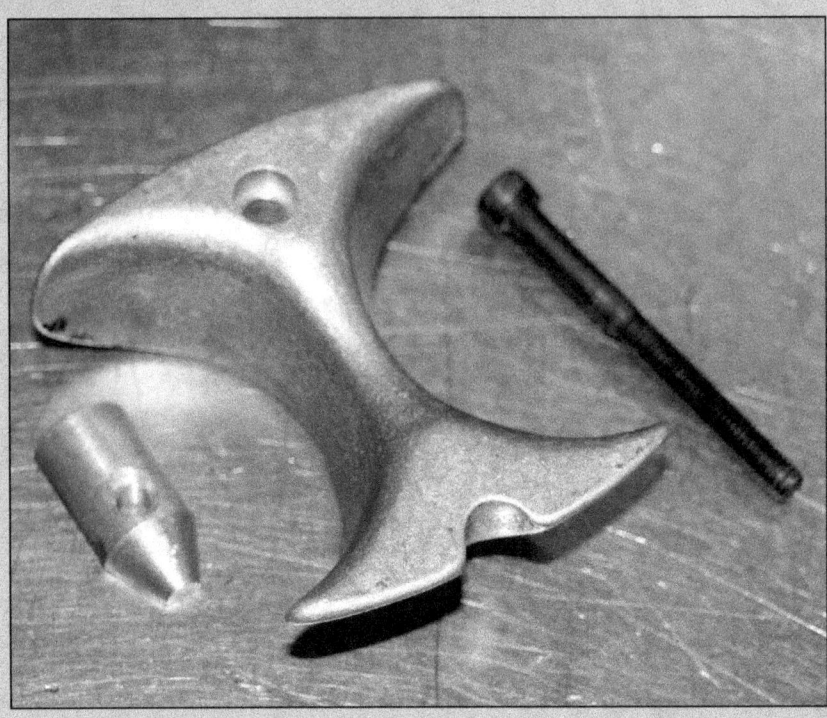

This little device fit all GM TPI/LT V-8s from 1985 to 1996. It is a very simple and elegant design. With more than 70,000 sold, it was one of the first emissions-era aftermarket components to be awarded an Executive Order (E.O.) by the California Air Resources Board (C.A.R.B.), making it legal in all states. It carries E.O. number 235-1.

others and the attention to detail that is necessary to achieve maximum performance.

TPIS markets the Airforce I and Airforce II filter housings. Chart D shows the airflow gain over a series of stock GM housings.

Chart A: Filter Lid to Throttle Body Airflow

Test	Airflow (cfm)
1. All stock, as factory delivered	434
2. Screens	out 512
2a. Airfoil installed	529
3. TPIS filter, Airfoil removed	529
4. Filter lid cut	555
5. Internally modified MAF sensor	569
6. Airfoil installed	585

Chart B: Airfoil Airflow

Test	Airflow (cfm)
7. Stock throttle body	668
8. Stock throttle body w/TPIS Airfoil	709

Chart C: MAF Airflow

Test	Airflow (cfm)
9. Stock MAF	529
10. MAF with screens removed	711
11. MAF with screens removed and internal surfaces smoothed	750

Chart D: Airflow

Component	CFM
Corvette Filter Housing A	719
Corvette Filter Housing B	712
Corvette Filter Housing C	704
Corvette Filter Housing D	685
Corvette Filter Housing E	631
TPIS Airforce I	890
TPIS Airforce II Modified Total CFM at 20.4	744

AIR AND FUEL MANAGEMENT

Chart E: Stock 350 TPI

	Without Airfoil		With Airfoil	
RPM	Corrected Brake Torque (ft-lbs)	Corrected Brake Horsepower	Corrected Brake Torque (ft-lbs)	Corrected Brake Horsepower
2,000	291.4	111.0	293.7 (+2.5)	111.9 (+.9)
2,250	295.5	126.6	297.8 (+2.3)	127.5 (+1.0)
2,500	305.0	145.2	308.5 (+3.5)	146.8 (+1.7)
2,750	315.8	165.4	318.6 (+2.8)	166.8 (+1.5)
3,000	325.8	186.1	327.4 (+1.6)	187.0 (+.9)
3,250	331.9	205.9	333.2 (+1.3)	206.2 (+.8)
3,500	332.6	221.6	333.2 (+.6)	222.0 (+.4)
3,750	326.6	233.2	328.5 (+1.9)	234.6 (+1.4)
4,000	317.6	241.5	318.5 (+1.4)	242.6 (+1.1)
4,250	302.9	245.1	306.5 (+3.6)	248.6 (+2.9)
4,500	284.6	243.8	289.6 (+5.0)	248.1 (+4.3)
4,750	259.0	234.2	266.2 (+7.2)	240.8 (+6.5)
5,000	235.5	224.2	240.4 (+4.9)	228.9 (+4.7)
5,250	210.5	210.4	215.4 (+4.9)	215.6 (+4.9)

Note: Numbers in parentheses ( ) indicte amount of change over first test.

Chart F: Fully Modified 350 TPI

	Without Airfoil		With Airfoil	
RPM	Corrected Brake Torque (ft-lbs)	Corrected Brake Horsepower	Corrected Brake Torque (ft-lbs)	Corrected Brake Horsepower
2,000	295.5	112.4	303.5 (+8.0)	115.6 (+3.2)
2,500	315.4	150.2	324.4 (+9.0)	154.5 (+4.3)
3,000	345.5	197.4	358.8 (+12.5)	204.6 (+7.2)
3,500	364.0	242.7	373.2 (+9.2)	248.8 (+4.6)
4,000	373.4	284.5	386.1 (+12.7)	294.2 (+9.7)
4,500	380.8	326.4	394.6 (+13.8)	338.2 (+11.8)
4,750	366.2	331.3	379.1 (+12.9)	343.1 (+11.8)
5,000	345.3	328.9	353.0 (+7.7)	336.4 (+7.5)

Note: Numbers in parentheses ( ) indicte amount of change over first test.

CHAPTER 5

The LT1 (in front) versus the LT4 (behind) intake gaskets. Notice the extra material added to the top of the LT4 intake manifold.

LT4 (upper) intake version and the LT1 (lower) version version. The difference is quite apparent.

again, make sure that you obtain the correct intake, as the Gen I, early-style intakes do not bolt on.

It is very important to note that the LT4 intake does, in fact, bolt onto a set of LT1 heads However, the ports do not match, and there is interference with the valve cover gasket rail on the LT1 heads.

Production Injectors

The 1992–1993 LT1 uses a 22-pound/hour injector, the 1994–1997 LT1 uses a 24-lbs/hr injector, and all LT4s use a 26-lbs/hr injector.

How to Size a Fuel Injector

When you increase your LT engine's power, it may require fuel injectors capable of flowing more fuel to adequately support the engine's new-found capability. Fuel injectors are offered in a wide range of sizes, and they are rated in pounds of fuel per hour that they are capable of flowing. This is represented as lbs/hr.

If you have a target horsepower number in mind, or if you are following the blueprint of another engine that has been built before (that you have horsepower figures for), you can use the following mathematical formula to determine the proper injector for your engine:

Injector Size = (horsepower X BSFC) ÷ (number of injectors x .8)

Where:
BSFC = brake specific fuel consumption

.8 represents the duty cycle of the injectors, since injectors can comfortably function at 80-percent duty for an extended period of time

As an example, let's use a 500-hp engine, running at .40 BSFC (which is within a normal range for an efficient engine), and using 8 injectors:

(500 x .4) ÷ (8 x .8)
200 ÷ 6.4
31.25 lbs/hr (per injector)

When purchasing injectors, you want to round up to the next higher number to ensure the injector you end up with has sufficient capabilities. Typical injector sizes jump are 24 lbs/hr, 36 lbs/hr, 42 lbs/hr, and 55 lbs/hr, so we'd choose 36 lbs/hr injectors for this particular engine.

Exhaust Headers

If you are serious about performance, exhaust headers are mandatory equipment. Factory exhaust manifolds are not very efficient, and upgrading to headers is a surefire way to gain power and performance throughout the RPM range. Freeing up the exhaust also contributes to improved fuel economy figures, due to improved efficiency.

It's generally understood that a long-tube header aids in lower-RPM power more than a comparable

AIR AND FUEL MANAGEMENT

This electronic control module (ECM) is the late style that can control two oxygen sensors.

This late ECM port is where the electronic spark control (ESC) is installed, which determines whether the motor is a six- or eight-cylinder. The ESC for the LT4 has a higher knock threshold and improves performance.

Early-style ECM, 1993 to 1994. Notice the large plugs, which are vastly different than the late style. This ECM uses only one oxygen sensor to manage fuel and air distribution.

short-tube header. It's also believed that a short primary tube length has a power advantage over the longer tubes at higher RPM. A properly-sized header helps throughout the RPM range, and determining the right length of header your engine wants before purchasing a set is a wise move.

So, how do you determine the best possible header diameter/length for your engine/application?

Header Length

Input the cubic-inch displacement of the engine for "CID." Input the maximum RPM of the engine into the equation. Input the Outside Diameter of the header tube for "OD" in the equation.

Multiply the CID by 1,900 and note the result.

Comparison of the two ECMs. In addition to the plug design, the boxes are different colors and made of different materials.

Speed/Density System versus

For the past several decades, we at TPIS have been working on programmable read-only memory (PROM) engine computer-chip programs. Ours differ from others on the market in several ways. We chose to address the more hardcore part of the market that's going to do more than install a thermostat. The first thing we did was test every PROM that General Motors has made for the 305- and 350-ci V-8 engines. What came as a big surprise were the vast differences in the calibrations. Even though the engines share basically the same hardware, we found a difference of 30 ft-lbs and 25 hp among factory PROM chips. Here are some details of what we found in the factory programming:

MAF System

This system is based on the mass airflow sensor as a means of sensing the volume of air the engine is consuming. In the original tuned port injection (TPI) system (offered on 305- and 350-ci V-8s from 1985 to 1989), the amount of fuel the engine received was determined by the MAF sensor. As the incoming engine air moved through the sensor, it passed over a wire that is electrically heated. As the incoming air cooled the wire, the computer sensed the change in resistance and added or subtracted fuel to maintain the proper air/fuel ratio.

The MAF sensor's ability to feed airflow information to the computer, the massive amount of stored ignition and drivability data, and the computer's learning ability make this system wonderfully adaptable.

Speed/Density System

As of 1990, General Motors adopted a Speed/Density fuel management system because it's less expensive to produce. This means it has removed the MAF sensor as the means of sensing the volume of air the engine is consuming. The Speed/Density system, through the manifold absolute pressure (MAP) sensor, electrically measures the pressure differences in the intake tract. As the pressure decreases, fuel is added, and vice versa.

The advantage of this system is that it reacts faster to RPM and load changes when set up properly. For racing applications, the Speed/Density system is the accepted way to go.

Racers can re-map their systems to maintain peak performance. In fact, some teams change the calibrations while the car is still on the track. This is done in the pits with a simple laptop, which is a major reason the MAP system is preferable.

The drawback to the Speed/Density system is that it must be programmed or mapped for each specific combination. Every camshaft, compression ratio, exhaust backpressure, and ignition alteration requires reprogramming.

When the calibrations are performed for a specific engine and driveline combination, the system works quite nicely. The problem is that there is very small latitude for change.

Differences

The only physical difference between the Mass Air Sensed system and the Speed/Density system is whether a MAF sensor or a MAP sensor is installed. The Speed/Density system has all the same components as the Mass Air Sensed system with the exception of the MAF sensor. Engine load is sensed by the MAP, as it is basically an

Mass airflow sensor (MAF) specifically for LT motors.

AIR AND FUEL MANAGEMENT

Mass Air Sensed System

electronic vacuum gauge. The computer refers to stored table data at specific RPM, throttle position, manifold pressure, and temperature settings to determine fuel and ignition requirements. The computer looks for a tachometer signal and sends the proper spark and fuel to each cylinder at the correct time. This calculation happens in fractions of a second, sending vital information with lightning-fast reactions. All of these calculations can be plotted on a three-dimensional graph, which looks very similar to a mountain range. These are called "maps."

Both systems deliver excellent performance as they were mapped by the factory on bone-stock engines. But when you change components such as intake runners or intake manifold, or add a performance improvement kit like the TPIS Fast Pack, the Speed/Density must be remapped.

The reality is General Motors leaves the system's programming on the rich side. The addition of performance pieces add airflow, and a nice performance gain is realized. As you add items that alter the vacuum characteristics of the engine, the MAP sensor doesn't know whether the engine is using more or less air. The MAP sensor does not have the authority to change the air/fuel ratio the way the Mass Air Sensed system does. Certainly, the engine's performance can be improved and the tuning maximized, but it requires a custom-programmed PROM to accurately reflect the changes in the engine. An adjustable fuel-pressure regulator is a more valuable tuning tool for the Speed/Density system than it is for the Mass Air Sensed system. So, if you have been paying attention carefully, if you take a planned approach to your build, you will find that the relatively simple Speed/Density system will reward you with positive performance gains.

Multiply the maximum engine RPM by the OD squared, and note the result.

Divide the first result by the second result to obtain the size of the pipe header.

$$\text{Header Tube Length} = (CID \times 1{,}900) \div (\text{peak RPM} \times \text{tube OD2})$$

Average Header Pipe Diameter(s)

Pipe diameter is determined by cubic-inch displacement and peak RPM.

There is a complex formula that can determine the optimal pipe diameter, but for LT1/LT4 engines, we only need to determine the best-possible choices for engines from 350 to 406 ci, spinning from 6,000 to 7,000 peak rpm.

Based on the headers offered for LT1-equipped cars, we can determine that 350-ci engines benefit from 1.5-inch head pipes, 383-ci engines benefit most from 1¾-inch head pipes, and 396-plus-ci engines need 2-inch-diameter head pipes.

These are based on 6,000-rpm redlines. Raising the RPM limit is justification for bumping up to the next larger pipe diameter offered.

Electronic Control Module

This is, of course, the dreaded "Black Box" of doom that strikes fear into the hearts of the bravest mechanics. Housed in an aluminum case, the "brains" of the electronic control module (ECM) house a variety of electric parts. The most well-known component of the ECM is the PROM (also called a chip). The ECM also contains a Cal Pak, or calibration package.

Many people are surprised to learn that the ECM has a "self-learn" capability. This allows the computer to make slight calibration tweaks to accommodate variations in operating conditions such as gasoline octane level, air temperature, and driving mode. One of the problems when testing new items for GM's TPI system is that all ECMs do not seem to learn at the same rate.

When making changes, you will be instructed to disconnect the battery. This is for many reasons, chiefly safety. This also clears (or "dumps") the ECM's memory of learned data. When power is reconnected, the ECM has to learn your driving habits all over again. When driving for the first time after power has been re-established, the vehicle may seem a little dead during part-throttle operation. It learns very quickly, so it doesn't take very long for a good portion of its final performance potential to return. We have found that this can occur as quickly as within 1 to 2 miles of driving. However, we have tested some vehicles that have

CHAPTER 5

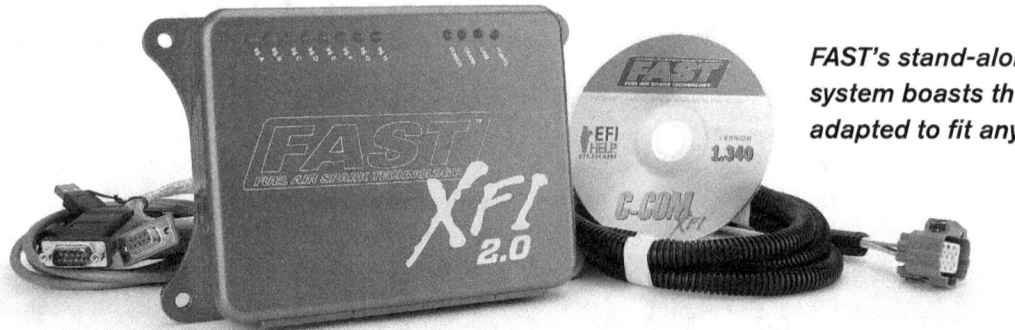

FAST's stand-alone fuel management system. The system boasts that it is self-learning and can be adapted to fit any motor with power adders.

EFI Sensors

All electronic fuel injection systems use an array of sensors and determine proper fuel and ignition settings based on information those sensors provide. Listed below are the typical sensors found in any electronic fuel injection system (including the LT1/4) and what they do.

Manifold Air Temperature Sensor (MAT)

This sensor is located in the intake ducting or as one of the functions of the MAF. Its job is to send air temperature data to the ECM.

Engine Coolant Temperature Sensor (ECT)

This sensor tells the ECM the temperature of the engine at any given time. It has more control over ECM functions than you might think. Because both ignition

Early L-98 screw with pintle compressed (top); late bolt in IAC with pintle extended (bottom).

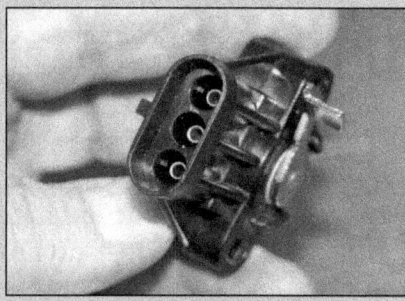

The 1985–1991 throttle position switch (TPS) has a flat, three-wire Weatherpac connector. This style of TPS can be used on an LT, but you need to change the connector from a round LT to the flat style shown here.

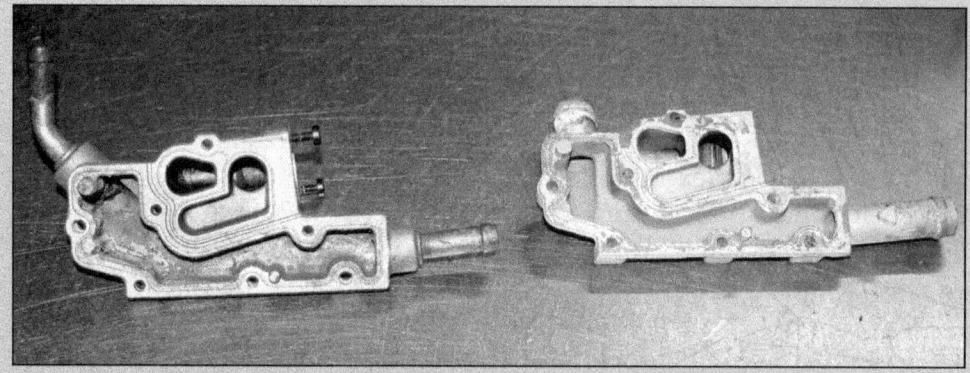

The idle air control housing, as found on LT engines. Late style is shown on the left; early style is shown on the right.

60   HOW TO BUILD MAX-PERFORMANCE CHEVY LT1/LT4 ENGINES

AIR AND FUEL MANAGEMENT

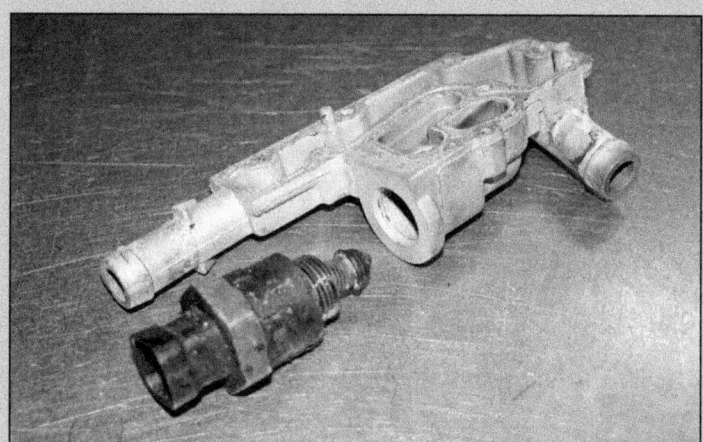
Another view of an early L-98 style IAC housing and motor.

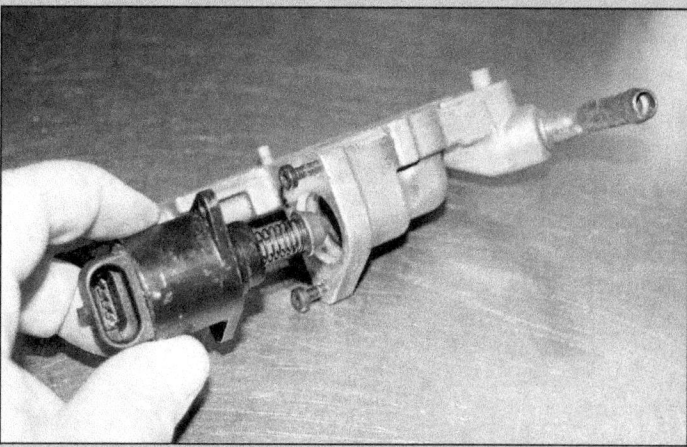
A late-style IAC housing and motor.

timing and the air/fuel ratio are adjusted according to coolant temperature, this sensor is vital to the health of the engine. Often the results of a failing coolant temperature sensor are poor fuel mileage and poor engine performance.

Idle Air Control (IAC)

This is a small electric stepper engine that gets its information from the ECM. The function of the idle air control (IAC) is to adjust the idle speed of the engine according to the engine load and temperature. It performs the job of a choke in a carbureted engine, allowing the engine to run a bit rich when it's first started until it achieves normal operating temperature.

Throttle Position Sensor (TPS)

This sensor tells the ECM the amount of throttle opening and the speed with which the throttle is being opened or closed (rate). The throttle position sensor (TPS) data is used to calculate the amount of air/fuel mixture enrichment needed during acceleration. In a carburetor this function is performed by the accelerator pump.

On the early (1985) TPI-equipped cars, the TPS is adjustable and a voltmeter is used to establish its position. The stock setting is .54 volt with the throttle closed. Rotating the TPS housing counterclockwise increases the voltage, similar to a potentiometer or dimming light switch. The higher the voltage, the richer the air/fuel mixture is and

Idle air control (IAC) motor installed on the throttle body.

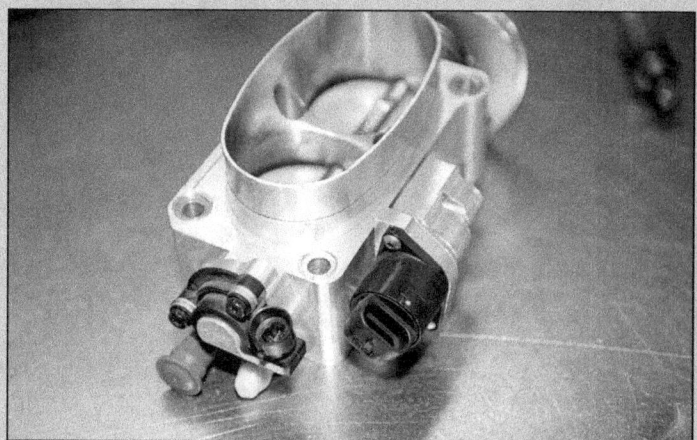
This photo shows the TPS and the IAC motor installed on the throttle body in relation to each other.

CHAPTER 5

EFI Sensors CONTINUED

This is the L-98 bolt pattern for a TPS.

This is the LT bolt pattern for a TPS.

typically, the better the throttle response. If you go too far you can get a "check-engine" light at idle. This normally illuminates as you cruise down the highway. You can raise the TPS voltage to about .64 before the check-engine light comes on. However, cars with the LT engine do not have an adjustable TPS.

Adjusting the TPS isn't necessary if you use any of the TPIS Magnum PROMs. You just leave it at the stock position, and we program the correct information into the PROM.

Manifold Absolute Pressure Sensor (MAP)

This sensor is essentially an electric vacuum gauge. As the pressure in the intake varies, the MAP sensor sends out different voltages to the ECM. The ECM then modifies the fuel curve accordingly.

A stock throttle body (bottom) and our version with an airfoil installed (top), usually good for a couple extra ponies.

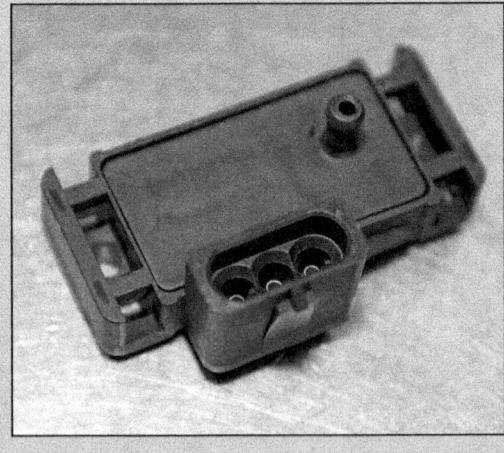

Manifold absolute pressure (MAP) sensor installed on the front of the intake manifold.

AIR AND FUEL MANAGEMENT

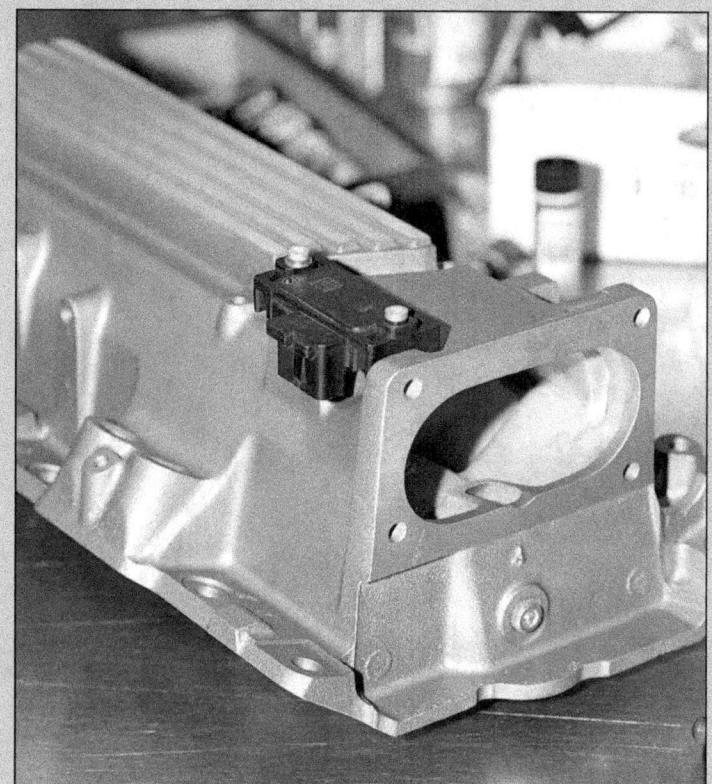

MAP sensor installed on the front and on top of the intake manifold.

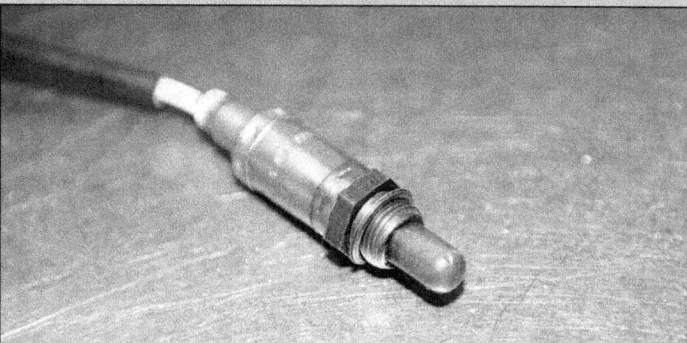

Typical GM oxygen sensor. Early-style motors had only one oxygen sensor, whereas the late-style had two oxygen sensors per the OBD II system government regulation.

Mass Airflow Sensor (MAF)

As mentioned earlier, the MAF measures the air volume to the cylinders by monitoring the electrical resistance in a heated wire as it is cooled by incoming air. More air flowing over the wire causes it to cool more, which then has less resistance. It sends this information to the ECM, which then adjusts fuel flow. It was used from 1985 to 1989, but General Motors chose to eliminate the MAF in the 1990–1991 350-ci- Camaro, Firebird, and Corvette engines. This was probably done for cost considerations because as emission regulations tightened General Motors went back to the mass air system in 1992 and has kept it right up to the current day.

Oxygen Sensor (EGO)

The oxygen sensor, also called an exhaust gas oxygen (EGO) sensor, monitors the oxygen level in the exhaust system. The ECM makes the necessary adjustments to keep the incoming mixture stoichiometric, which is the chemically ideal air/fuel ratio of 14.7:1.

On some installations, where the oxygen sensor is located on the aftermarket exhaust headers, you probably want to use a heated sensor. This is done so the EFI system goes into "closed loop" operation mode (which is more accurate and therefore preferred) sooner. TPIS offers a three-wire heated sensor that is compatible with the GM TPI systems.

Early LT1 fuel-injection systems had only one oxygen sensor, while later systems had two. This was due to the government's mandating of the OBD-II engine management systems. Systems with two oxygen sensors have one "upstream" and one "downstream." This refers to exhaust flow before and after the catalytic converter, respectively. This way, the two oxygen sensors can compare their readings and measure the effectiveness of the catalytic converter.

Knock Sensor

Engine knock sensors were installed on all years of LT1/LT4 engines. This sensor acts a microphone that hears the combustion process and sends danger signals to the ECM when it detects a detonation knock or a ping. The ECM momentarily retards the ignition timing when a knock or ping is detected. Engines made in various years use different knock sensors, so be sure to use the correct one for your application/ECM.

CHAPTER 5

EFI Sensors CONTINUED

B-Body and Y-Body cars use two knock sensors. The 1992–1995 models use one part number while the 1996–1997 models use another part number.

- B-Body is a Caprice/Impala SS
- F-Body is a Camaro or Firebird
- Y-Body is a Corvette

Exhaust Gas Recirculation Valve

The EGR valve is a small device found on the rear of the intake manifold. This is an emissions-control piece that helps the engine burn fuel more efficiently by recirculating a portion of the exhaust and having it go through the combustion process again. This results in a cooler, more complete burn of the fuel, which decreases noxious emissions. Most rough-idle conditions and poor-acceleration problems can be traced back to the EGR valve. Exhaust gases are dirty, and repeated exposure to them tends to corrode and/or clog these valves. Once they're not functioning correctly, the engine's air/fuel mix may be impacted and it cannot run effectively. The EGR valve is almost always suspect when an LT1/LT4 engine with some mileage suddenly begins running rough.

Here are pictured three different knock sensors.

The LT4 had more overlap (the time when both the intake and exhaust valves are open) in its camshaft, which dilutes the intake charge with exhaust. In effect, this acts as its own EGR. Therefore, the LT4 did not need an external EGR valve. The LT4 intakes were furnished with a factory block-off plate. For example, if you chose to run one of our ZZ9 cams in your LT1, you do not need to run an EGR valve on your engine for this very reason.

not reached their full potential for 50 to 75 miles! It all depends on which ECM you have.

It deserves to be mentioned that newer ECMs (both factory and aftermarket) have much faster learning functions. As computing power has increased in these engine control units, the time they take to "learn" has decreased in kind.

Let us reiterate a major point: When you have a road test after a modification such as an airfoil, adjustable fuel pressure regulator, air filter, spark plug wires, PROMs, or others, you definitely see gains immediately, but it may take time to realize their full potential. There have been a few reports from drivers who can feel gains of .10 second in the 1/4-mile. We all become accustomed to the performance of our cars, so minor differences may not be noticed immediately. Additionally, it always helps to have the proper testing equipment to keep an objective eye.

There are five basic ECU part numbers for the LT1/LT4 engine family. We typically use the last three or four digits of the full part number to identify a given ECU. As an example, a 1992–1993 Corvette ECU part number is 16163993, but we would call it a 3993. A 1994–1995 F-Body uses an 8051 ECU; a 1994–1995 Corvette uses a 133. For 1996–1997 a B-Body uses a 4399 ECU; an F-Body uses a 921 ECU; and the Y-Body is 2148. You get the idea. Each of these ECUs has its own characteristics.

Modes of ECU Operation

There are three basic modes of operation: limp home, open loop, and closed loop. They all apply to both Mass Air Sensed and Speed/Density systems.

Limp Home

This mode is designed to get you home in the event of a major system or sensor malfunction. It is also the mode that street rodders tend to use

AIR AND FUEL MANAGEMENT

409 LTI GM Stock Intake vs. TPIS MiniRam

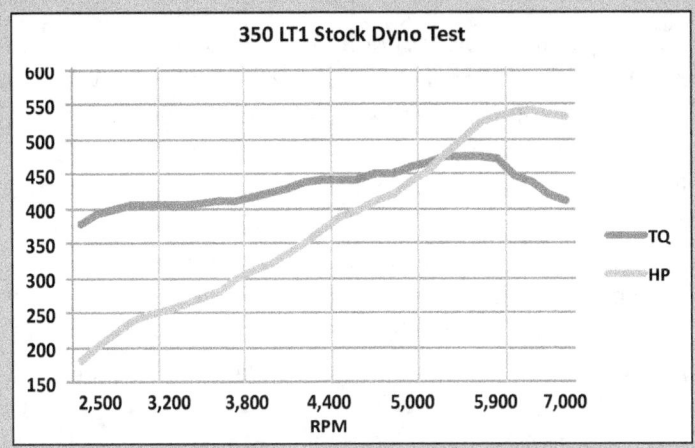

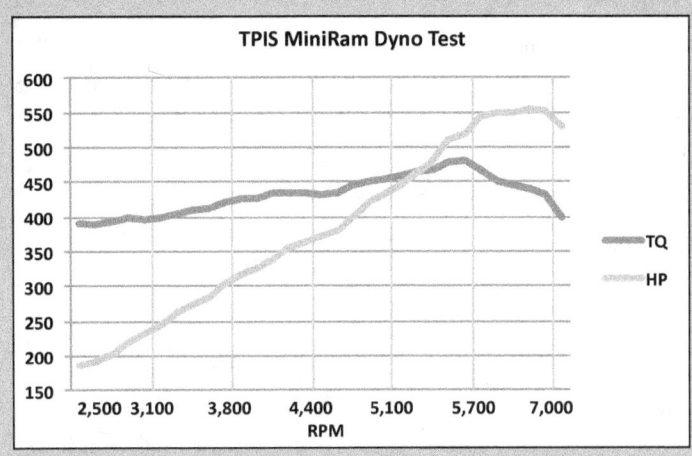

RPM	TQ	HP	RPM	TQ	HP	RPM	TQ	HP	RPM	TQ	HP
2,500	377.9	179.9	4,800	451.1	412.3	2,500	390.9	186.1	4,800	449.2	410.5
2,600	383.6	189.9	4,900	451.7	421.4	2,600	389.2	192.7	4,900	449.9	419.7
2,700	393.1	202.1	5,000	460.3	438.2	2,700	393.0	202.0	5,000	452.8	431.1
2,800	397.1	211.7	5,100	466.4	452.9	2,800	395.9	211.1	5,100	458.9	445.6
2,900	400.4	221.1	5,200	467.7	463.1	2,900	398.4	220.0	5,200	466.0	461.4
3,000	402.5	229.9	5,300	473.9	478.2	3,000	398.0	227.3	5,300	465.8	470.1
3,100	404.9	239.0	5,400	476.7	490.1	3,100	396.6	234.1	5,400	466.7	479.9
3,200	406.3	247.6	5,500	476.1	498.6	3,200	399.2	243.2	5,500	**483.7**	506.5
3,300	405.4	254.7	5,600	480.9	512.8	3,300	400.3	251.5	5,600	479.1	510.8
3,400	404.2	261.7	5,700	**483.4**	524.6	3,400	404.3	261.7	5,700	479.7	520.6
3,500	409.7	273.0	5,800	475.2	524.8	3,500	409.8	273.1	5,800	478.6	528.5
3,600	411.8	282.3	5,900	473.7	532.1	3,600	413.9	283.7	5,900	474.6	533.2
3,700	411.7	290.0	6,000	463.2	529.2	3,700	419.7	295.7	6,000	470.3	537.3
3,800	412.8	298.7	6,100	458.9	533.0	3,800	421.1	304.7	6,100	467.3	542.8
3,900	418.6	310.8	6,200	452.9	534.6	3,900	425.6	316.0	6,200	463.3	546.9
4,000	423.1	322.2	6,300	449.6	539.3	4,000	427.8	325.8	6,300	453.9	544.5
4,100	429.2	335.1	6,400	441.7	538.2	4,100	434.4	339.1	6,400	450.1	548.5
4,200	439.1	351.1	6,500	438.8	**543.1**	4,200	434.3	347.3	6,500	444.8	550.5
4,300	441.0	361.1	6,600	427.8	537.6	4,300	434.6	355.8	6,600	441.4	**554.7**
4,400	440.8	369.3	6,700	420.7	536.7	4,400	433.4	363.1	6,700	432.4	551.6
4,500	440.4	377.3	6,800	410.5	531.5	4,500	432.7	370.7	6,800	421.7	546.0
4,600	442.5	387.6	6,900	401.3	527.2	4,600	434.4	380.5	6,900	404.2	531.0
4,700	443.1	396.5	7,000	390.7	520.7	4,700	445.0	398.2	7,000	398.6	531.3

CHAPTER 5

409 LTI GM Stock Intake vs. TPIS MiniRam CONTINUED

Displacement	409 ci
Block	GM, 4-bolt with splayed cap
Pistons	Diamond, 4.100
Camshaft	TPIS ZZ-X
Intake/Exhaust (degrees)	239/239
Lift (inches)	.050
Intake/Exhaust Valve Lift (inches)	.558/.558
Centerline (degrees)	110
Rods	Manley pro 5.850
Heads	GM, LT-4 (I ported these myself)
Oil Pan	Canton road race
Throttle Body	TPIS, 58 mm
Crankshaft	Callies, 3.875 stroke
Timing Chain	Cloyes
Intake	GM vs TPIS
Ignition	Optispark with MSD 6AL
Compression Ratio	11:1

This test is a comparison of a stock LT1 intake and a TPIS MiniRam intake. As you can see, there is a dramatic improvement in power production. This engine is used in my (Myron's) personal 1954 Chevy Sedan Delivery, which is a true pump-gas street machine designed to perform more like a modern car. It has many suspension upgrades for improved handling and braking performance, and the addition of this late-model computer-controlled engine only improves the roadworthiness of the car.

For many years we felt that the improvement offered by installing a TPIS Mini-Ram on a near-stock 350-ci LT1 would result only in small, upper-RPM gains. Well, this test surprised us with its results. Where Build #6 (page 121) is a large-displacement, high-compression (11.5:1), large-camshaft (242 duration) combination we knew could benefit from the MiniRam's big plenum and short runner length design, the engine for this test is simply a port-matched 1994 350-ci powerplant out of my (Myron) emissions-legal Camaro with a ZZ-9 camshaft. The gains realized from 2,300 to 4,000 rpm are going to be very satisfying on the road, and this experiment showed us that the MiniRam is more versatile than we gave it credit for. The engine found its way into my (Myron) Sedan Delivery, and has proven to be a reliable performer for the past few years.

---

because of improper wiring. In limp-home mode, the TPS controls the fuel curve much like a Hilborn injector, and the timing is fixed at about 22 degrees total. This is not very efficient but it does maintain drivability and allows you to get home or to a repair shop if you have problems. The TPIS Adjustable Fuel Pressure Regulator is most helpful in improving the performance of engines running in limp-home mode.

Open Loop

This means that the system is not under the control of the oxygen sensor. This occurs during warm up and during wide-open-throttle (WOT) operations. The system uses spark and fuel tables that have been programmed into the PROM or the memory of the ECU.

Closed Loop

This occurs when the oxygen has come up to temperature (about 600 degrees F) and is providing a signal back to the ECM. This is the mode that makes the TPI so nice to drive. Good throttle response, great idle, and good gas mileage all happen once the engine enters closed-loop operation and can rely on its programming.

Closed-loop operations are effective only during idle and part-throttle operation. At wide-open throttle, the ECM automatically switches to open-loop mode.

Throttle position sensor (TPS) installed on the billet throttle body. This is an easy swap that provides increased airflow.

Supercharging and Turbos

There are many things to consider if you are going to add a supercharger or turbo kit. The additional pressures involved bring greater stresses to critical areas within the engine, but these challenges can be overcome. All it takes is some careful considerations and strategic investments to ensure the engine is capable of withstanding the greater cylinder pressures created through the use of either a supercharger or nitrous oxide injection. The specific upgrades for each are different in some ways and the same in others.

In the short block, the boost level dictates the ring package. If boost pressure will be 10 pounds or less at peak pressure, we recommend upgrading to a quality moly-coated top piston ring, a cast-iron second ring, and a stainless-steel oil ring.

Optimally, the whole ring package is moved down on the piston. This serves several purposes. First, the top ring is farther away from the heat of the chamber. Use of a supercharger (to create boost) or nitrous oxide (to burn more fuel) increases the heat and pressure in the combustion chamber, and the ring benefits from any distance that can be added here.

Also, moving the ring down on the piston allows the piston deck to be thicker before it must be cut for the top ring groove. The thicker deck is not only stronger, but also capable of dealing with greater heat, as the forged aluminum can absorb and disperse it more effectively than a comparable thin-deck piston. Specifying the lower ring groove location needs to be done at the time the pistons are ordered, as typical (non-supercharged/nitrous) high-performance pistons are designed to be as lightweight as possible, with the rings pushed toward the chamber more than a comparable factory piston. This minimizes the "dirty" area directly over the ring, resulting in a cleaner, more efficient burn in a non-boosted application. We also recommend having the pistons coated. The results are worth the effort. In most cases, the piston domes are given a thermal heat barrier, while their skirts are treated with a graphite-based low-friction modifier.

As you raise the boost level beyond 10 psi, some design changes should take place. The top ring gets changed to a ductile steel material, as this type of ring takes more abuse from the heat and the extreme cylinder pressure caused by detonation. Additionally, we recommend specifying a thicker-wall piston wrist pin for increased strength and durability (at the expense of increased weight); these pins should be casidium coated to minimize friction in the high-heat environment.

As for the cylinder heads running at the lower (10-psi peak) boost level, you need to raise the seat pressure on the intake valvespring. The reason for is: Unless you compensate for the supercharger boost pressure on the back of the valve, you may experience premature valve float. This can lead to a backfire or worse. A backfire alone can be very damaging to gaskets, seals, and throttle blades along the intake tract. An intake valve that's slow to close (due to the combination of a weak spring and boost pressure trying to keep it open) may make contact with the upward-travelling piston, which bends the valve and causes more damage.

To calculate how much to increase the spring pressure, simply add 1 percent to your existing valvespring rating. For example, if your valvespring is rated at 300 pounds (at installed height), you want to upgrade to a 305-pound spring.

CHAPTER 6

IGNITION AND ELECTRONIC CONTROLS

The ignition in the LT series of engines is unique. If you're used to the typical rear-mounted distributor, this is a great departure from convention. The distributor is mounted directly to the timing chain cover and driven by the front of the camshaft via a short driveshaft (on the early engine) or a pin drive (on the later LT1). The Optispark unit is located behind the water pump, which is also driven by the camshaft gear. This system uses a light-and-diode system that functions as a trigger to provide for each cylinder's perfectly timed spark and injection events. Unfortunately, this system, while innovative, was wholly flawed by reliability issues.

LT distributor from the back of the engine. This is a 1992–1994 version with the keyed driveshaft.

Optispark

The distributor cap on the early versions of the Optispark (until 1995) were not vented. Since 1995, they were vented via a vacuum hose connected to the distributor cap. This hose is connected to a vacuum port on the intake manifold. The second vacuum port on the cap connects to the intake ducting. This provides airflow through the distributor, hopefully purging moisture. The trigger wheel of the Optispark has 360 slots, and these properly index the firing order and fuel injection sequence. They are known as the reference, or REF. A smaller radius of four slots exists inside them. The inner four slots synchronize the computer to tell it when to fire the number-1 cylinder, and are known as the SYNC.

The Optispark certainly is the weak point of the redesign. In our humble opinion General Motors had several better choices of engine management systems to choose from. The fact that GM engineers were working on the new LS engine in the mid 1990s means they could have

IGNITION AND ELECTRONIC CONTROLS

upgraded the LT. Enthusiasts like us sure wish they would have!

Removing and replacing the Optispark system is a very labor-intensive endeavor. This is chiefly due to the fact that the water pump must be removed in order to access the distributor. This requires draining the entire cooling system, which is messy and adds extra cost to an already relatively major repair. The firing order is the same as on all Chevy V-8s from 1955 to 1991: 1-8-4-3-6-5-7-2. The one advantage to the Optispark is that the cap is designed and wired in such a way that all the odd-numbered wires are on the left side and the even-numbered wires are on the right. This makes wire routing neat and simple. It also puts the ignition behind the water pump and relatively low on the front of the engine, where it can easily get wet in a wide range of situations. This has traditionally been the weak point of the LT-series ignition system, and has given an unfair reputation for unreliability to the entire line of engines in the eyes of many.

Ignition Coil

This ignition system utilizes a single coil mounted on the cylinder head. Which cylinder head is used depends upon which vehicle it was installed on. It has a preinstalled coil driver, which limits the amperage that the coil can produce. Again, this type of system is very limiting when it comes to power output, both the output of the coil and the output from the engine itself. Aftermarket options (such as those from MSD) can improve the coil's output.

Wiring Harness

The stock harness that came in production vehicles has proven to be perfectly adequate for street, strip, and road race use. It's well designed and the connectors are weatherproof. If you are going to install an LT1/LT4 V-8 into a project car that was not equipped with one, you'd be well served to get an aftermarket wire harness from Painless Performance, TPIS, Howell Engineering or other reliable source.

Although the factory harnesses can be used in engine swaps, they include a lot of supplemental vehicle wiring that is not related to the engine. Naturally, all of these unnecessary wires should be removed from the harness before it is installed, and the effort required to do this effectively is great.

Aftermarket harnesses are designed specifically to run the engine and nothing more, so they are much more compact and effectively labeled to facilitate such engine swaps. They're also clean, since they're new. Salvaged harnesses are not labeled, and are typically filthy. This makes them a lot less of a joy to work with, since every wire has to be researched and tested to ensure its worthiness. New harnesses require none of this effort.

Small driveshaft that drives the distributor. This is the first (1992–1994) design that has a keyway and is easily pressed into place. Do not force it! You can easily damage the teeth, as can be seen in the close-up of the gears themselves. Subsequent versions of the LT distributor do not have this feature.

CHAPTER 6

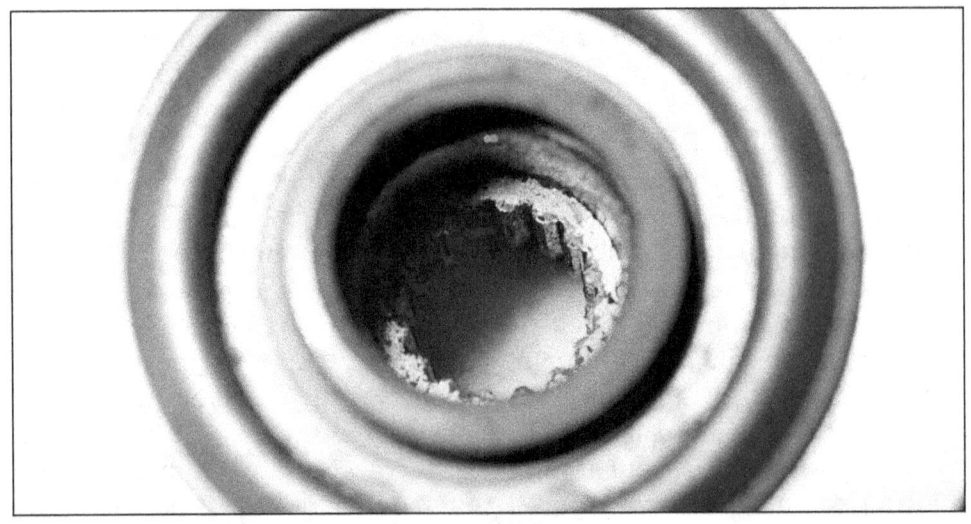

Up-close look at the keyway with rounded teeth, proof that someone has tried to force this piece into place.

Crank position sensor for the OBDII fuel management system.

Early-style LT distributor with keyed driveshaft removed (left) Late style is shown on the right.

IGNITION AND ELECTRONIC CONTROLS

Distributor side gear with keyway.

Late-style distributor with pressed-in drive seal. Do not pry this piece off; it will break the distributor.

Late-style distributor vacuum port, which allows filtered air to be drawn into the distributor to keep it dry. This can be capped if not being used.

Late-style distributor with indication of where the long pin is supposed to be placed. Any other installation of the camshaft pin results in a poorly timed motor or a motor that does not fire.

An easy way to tell the difference between the early-model and the late-model distributors is the color and depth of the plug. The early style (above) uses a black plug that is shallow. The late style (bottom) uses a white plug that is much deeper.

IGNITION AND ELECTRONIC CONTROLS

Photo showing the mating of the camshaft and the late-style distributor. This step is crucial to making it match up properly.

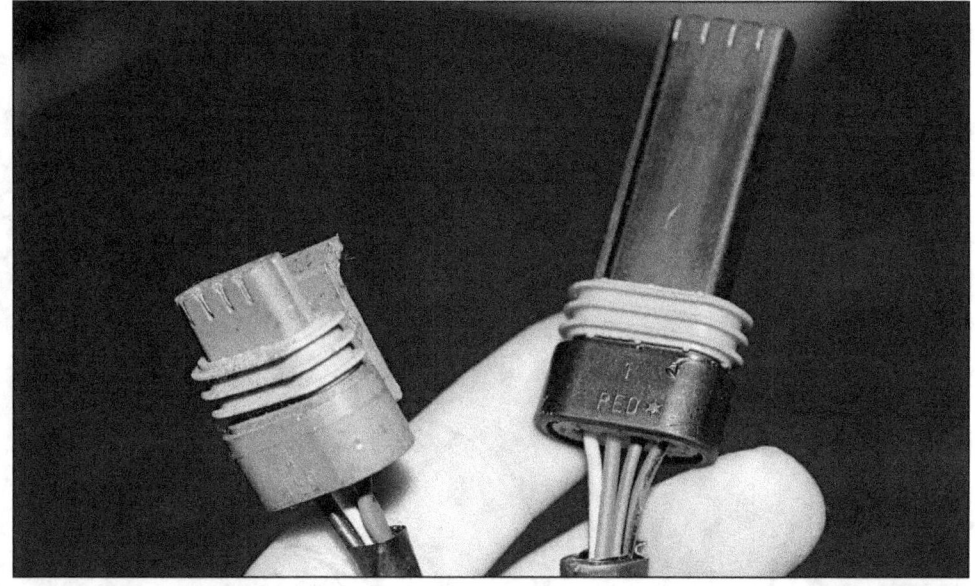

There are two different styles of Optispark connectors: one shallow and one deep.

Here are the two different pigtails for the distributors. In order to swap distributors between early and late versions, you must cut off the terminals and splice the corresponding wires correctly. Once again, the short style is the early version of the distributor and the long style is the late version. The color of the plug also helps identify them.

CHAPTER 6

The 24X System

The 24X system allows you to run the more reliable and more powerful LS-style coils on your LT engine. It is vastly superior to the stock system, but with that comes a high price. This conversion isn't as simple as slapping a set of coil packs on your engine, it takes careful planning and the usage of a newer-style LS ECM to properly employ the coil packs.

We have dyno tests with the 24X system (see Chapter 8) that show huge gains over the archaic Optispark system. We have seen as much as 25 hp and 25 ft-lbs of torque by doing this one modification alone. It's well worth the effort and cost.

1 *This is the appropriate tool for the removal and installation of the LT1/LT4 crankshaft hub. Do yourself a huge favor and find a used one, use it, and then re-sell it. This kit makes removal of the unusual LT engine crank hub both safe and easy.*

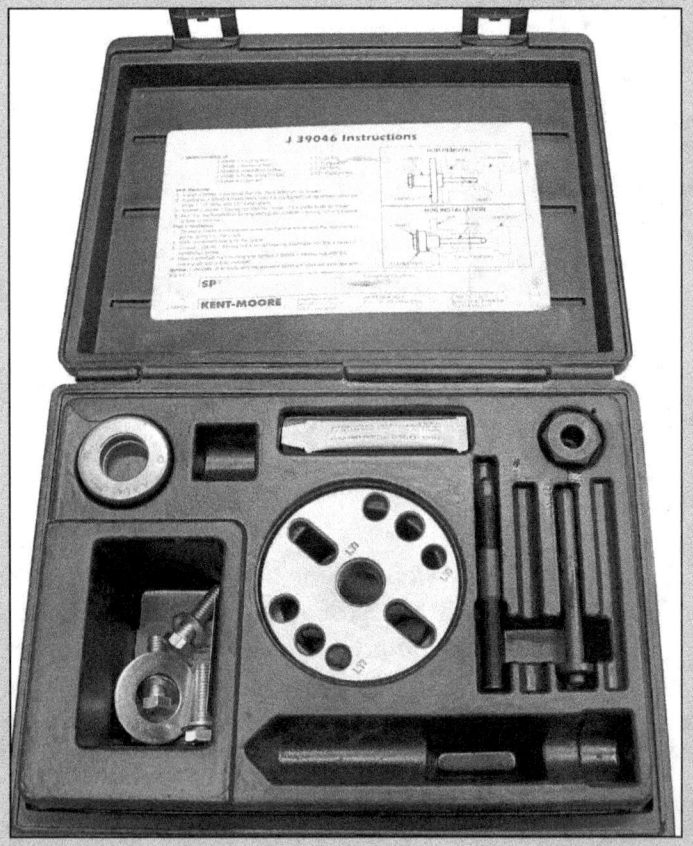

2 *The kit contains all the necessary tools to properly remove and install the hub. You can see the detailed directions on the use of the tool permanently affixed to the lid of the case. If you've ever used a balancer puller, this procedure should be familiar. Be sure to follow the directions to ensure no damage occurs to the hub or the crankshaft. Damage to the crankshaft requires its removal to repair or replace it, and that's a lot more work and expense than this job requires.*

IGNITION AND ELECTRONIC CONTROLS

3 Unbolt the balancer. Insert the removal bar into the crankshaft end. Obviously, the engine will have to be disassembled partially prior to this work being performed. (Also, while you'll see that we are accomplishing this on an engine that's been removed from the vehicle, this is only so you can clearly see the process.) It's entirely possible to do this with the engine still in the car.

4 Assemble the puller body onto the crank hub using the bolts and washers included in the kit. Do not tighten any of the bolts until all three of them have been installed. Then, tighten them evenly to ensure the puller body is properly installed.

5 Thread the forcing nut into the puller body. Prevent the crankshaft from turning, and tighten the forcing nut until the hub is removed. You can use an air-powered impact gun, which works quickly and effectively. You can also use hand tools, but it takes a lot longer.

CHAPTER 6

The 24X System CONTINUTED

6 Using the proper tools make removing the hub a simple process.

7 Remove the oil pan bolts and the front oil pan nuts, and loosen the rear oil pan nuts. The front of the oil pan drops enough to give you plenty of clearance to remove the timing cover assembly.

8 Remove the timing cover. You should see the factory four-tooth crank reluctor if the engine is a 1996–1997 LT1/LT4. Remove the LT1 crank reluctor by gently prying on it with a large screwdriver.

IGNITION AND ELECTRONIC CONTROLS

9 *Install the EFI Connection 24X crank reluctor in place of the factory unit. It should sit flush.*

10 *The 1995–1997 LT1 engines have an extended dowel pins in the camshaft to turn the factory Optispark distributor. The earlier 1992–1994 LT1 engines have a shorter dowel pin on the cam, as did the earlier small-block Chevys.*

The 24X System *CONTINUED*

11 Notice how far this longer camshaft dowel pin extends through the EFI Connection cam reluctor. This dowel pin must be shortened (or just tapped into the cam farther) to gain adequate clearance for the cam sensor housing. (This step is not required on the earlier 1992–1994 LT1 camshafts or on aftermarket hydraulic roller camshafts.)

12 With the new reluctor in place, draw a line on the long dowel pin to mark where it will be cut. While it's possible to tap the pin in farther in some cases, this can sometimes cause more problems than it's worth. The pin itself is made of a very soft metal that tends to mushroom when it's hammered too hard, so if possible, just cut it. You can use a simple cut-off wheel or even a hacksaw or band saw.

13 Once cut, reinstall the dowel pin into the camshaft.

IGNITION AND ELECTRONIC CONTROLS

14 *The new reluctor is installed with button-head hex-head bolts. Be sure to use liquid thread-locker, such as Loctite, to secure the fasteners in place and torque them to proper specification. The GM Service Manual calls for 18 ft-lbs.*

15 *Install the cam sensor housing where the factory Optispark unit was previously. A GM Gen VI LS cam sensor is installed into the cam sensor housing to pick up a signal from the reluctor bolted to the camshaft.*

The 24X System CONTINUED

16 Begin the installation of the coil bracket assemblies by removing the original valve cover bolts.

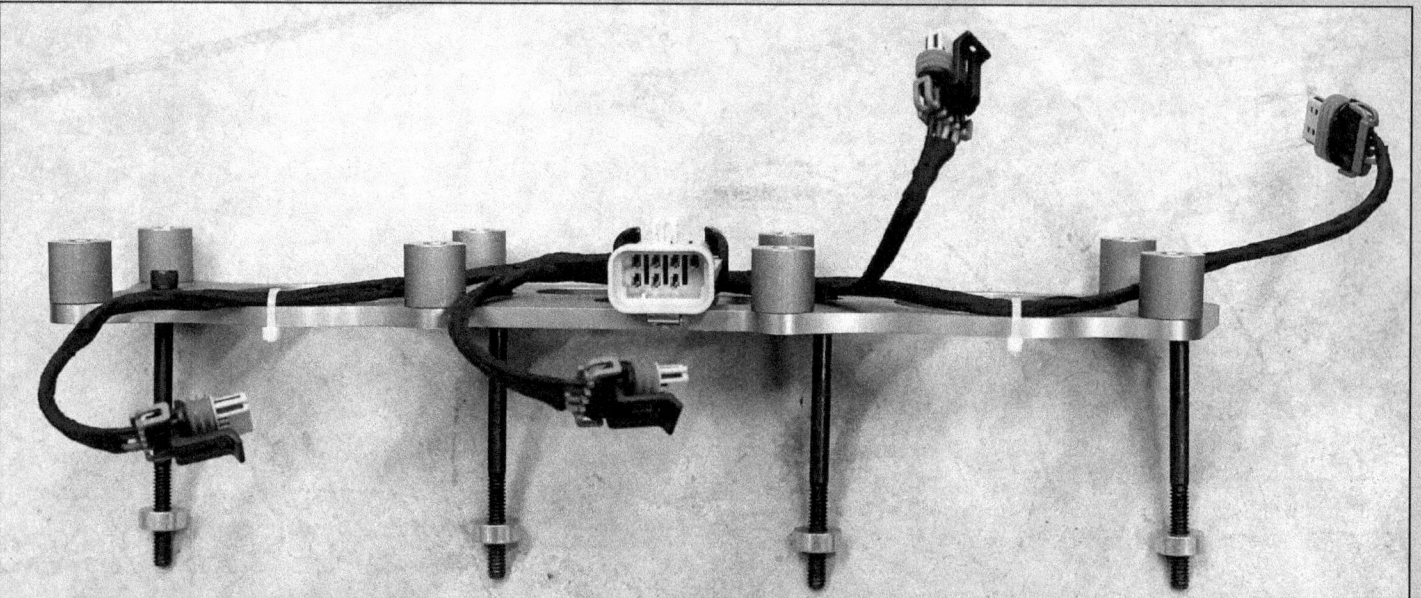

17 Remove the ignition coils from the bracket. Pre-assemble the 3¾-inch-long socket-head bolts and 1/4-inch aluminum spacers as shown. The bracket is slightly elevated from the valve cover by the spacers.

IGNITION AND ELECTRONIC CONTROLS

18 Sandwich the 1/4-inch spacers between the bracket and the valve cover.

19 Tighten the four socket-head bolts evenly to secure the bracket assembly to the valve cover. Repeat this procedure on the other side of the engine.

20 Install the ignition coils on the brackets using the provided socket-head fasteners. Plug the wiring harness into each respective ignition coil.

21 This LT1 long-block assembly is now ready to run the EFI Connection 24X engine control system once the wiring harness is plugged in. With the addition of an intake manifold and its belt-driven accessories, it will be complete.

John Schaefer 383 LT1 Optispark vs. LS1 24X

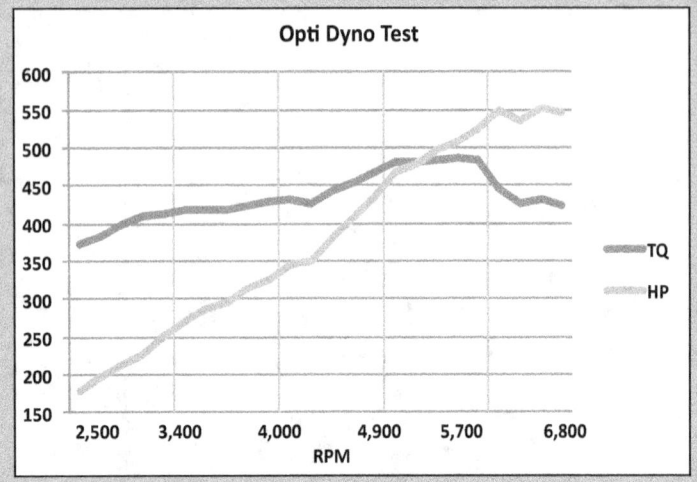

RPM	TQ	HP	RPM	TQ	HP	RPM	TQ	HP	RPM	TQ	HP
2,500	372.7	177.4	4,700	454.0	406.2	2,500	406.0	193.3	4,700	480.3	429.8
2,600	377.1	186.7	4,800	461.3	421.6	2,600	406.7	201.3	4,800	480.0	438.7
2,700	383.5	197.2	4,900	467.2	435.9	2,700	413.9	212.8	4,900	489.4	456.6
2,800	398.8	212.6	5,000	479.6	456.6	2,800	421.3	224.6	5,000	496.7	472.9
2,900	410.9	226.9	5,100	482.1	468.2	2,900	424.0	234.1	5,100	493.1	478.8
3,000	413.4	236.1	5,200	482.4	477.6	3,000	424.5	242.5	5,200	503.2	498.2
3,100	410.7	242.4	5,300	483.9	488.3	3,100	424.6	250.6	5,300	**506.7**	511.3
3,200	412.2	251.2	5,400	482.6	496.1	3,200	426.3	259.7	5,400	502.6	516.8
3,300	413.1	259.6	5,500	485.6	508.5	3,300	430.7	270.6	5,500	502.1	525.8
3,400	417.6	270.4	5,600	**486.6**	518.8	3,400	428.5	277.4	5,600	499.2	532.3
3,500	419.0	279.2	5,700	483.5	524.7	3,500	430.0	286.5	5,700	496.4	538.7
3,600	418.4	286.8	5,800	473.6	523.0	3,600	437.4	299.8	5,800	494.3	545.9
3,700	418.6	294.9	5,900	467.9	525.6	3,700	441.1	310.8	5,900	494.9	555.9
3,800	424.8	307.4	6,000	462.5	528.4	3,800	445.8	322.5	6,000	489.4	559.1
3,900	423.6	314.6	6,100	462.8	537.5	3,900	446.0	331.2	6,100	480.3	557.9
4,000	428.6	326.4	6,200	454.2	536.2	4,000	447.8	341.1	6,200	475.6	561.5
4,100	424.8	331.6	6,300	456.3	547.4	4,100	442.9	345.7	6,300	466.1	559.1
4,200	431.0	344.7	6,400	450.4	548.9	4,200	441.9	353.4	6,400	459.3	559.7
4,300	426.9	349.5	6,500	444.3	549.9	4,300	454.5	372.1	6,500	454.2	562.1
4,400	425.6	356.6	6,600	425.9	535.2	4,400	456.4	382.4	6,600	450.6	**566.3**
4,500	442.7	379.3	6,700	432.9	**552.2**	4,500	461.4	395.3	6,700	443.5	565.7
4,600	451.5	395.5	6,800	422.7	547.2	4,600	467.7	409.6	6,800	432.1	559.4

IGNITION AND ELECTRONIC CONTROLS

OBDI LT1 PCM

Displacement	383 ci
Block	Stock with splayed caps
Pistons	Diamond, .030 over
Camshaft	TPIS 242 solid roller
Intake/Exhaust (degrees)	242/242
Lift (inches)	.050
Intake/Exhaust Valve Lift (inches)	.558/.558
Centerline (degrees)	112
Rods	Callies Compstar, 6 inch
Heads	AFR 210-cc Comp Port
Oil Pan	Canton road race
Throttle Body	TPIS Monoblade
Crankshaft	Callies
Timing Chain	Cloyes
Intake	MiniRam LT
Ignition	GM Optispark with MSD 6AL
Compression Ratio	11.2:1
Ignition	Delphi 5 Wire MAF, 90-mm, 36-pound injectors at 60 psi, EFI connection

24X

Displacement	383 ci
Block	Stock with splayed caps
Pistons	Diamond, .030 over
Camshaft	TPIS 242 solid roller
Rods	Callies Compstar, 6 inch
Heads	AFR 210-cc competition port
Oil Pan	Canton road race
Throttle Body	Monoblade
Crankshaft	Callies
Timing Chain	Cloyes
Intake	MiniRam LT
Ignition	24X
Compression Ratio	11.2:1
Ignition	Delphi 5 Wire MAF, 90-mm, 36-pound injectors at 60 psi, EFI Connection 24X system

This is a back-to-back comparison of two different ignition systems. The first is a factory Optispark ignition with an MSD 6AL box and a TPIS coil. This MSD-enhanced factory ignition is how we've run the LT1/LT4 engines we've built for years. It was better than the factory produced it, but still had some long-term durability and misfire issues. This was especially true in wet weather and very harsh racing environments. It wasn't unheard of for a car not to start after being washed, for example. Our upgrades and modifications made that a lot better, but still couldn't completely cure the design's shortcomings.

The second part of the test is with a completely redesigned engine management system, utilizing a new electrical harness and ECU based on the GM LS-series engine's ignition components. This setup eliminates the Optispark distributor and all of its associated problems.

Look at the two back-to-back runs to see a surprise. This not an inexpensive upgrade, but the gains are dramatic. Before we ran this test, you could not get us to believe that the factory LT1 spark output was deficient. But here's the test. We have redone it several times, and have always seen the same result. This is one of the best upgrades you can accomplish with your LT1/LT4 engine.

It's also interesting to look at power per cubic inch and torque per cubic inch:

	Optispark	*24X*
HP/ci	1.44	1.47
Torque/ci	1.26	1.32

CHAPTER 7

ASSEMBLY

When assembling an engine, a certain sequence needs to be followed. Don't make any assumptions, as every detail must be checked.

Let's start with your expectations, power-wise, budget-wise. You must remain realistic, as a 700-hp nitrous bullet with cast pistons and stock rods is not going to enhance your image at the race track when it comes apart in spectacular fashion.

The smart thing to do is to build an LT-based engine that is capable of driving to the track, racing for the day, and then driving home. The most popular sizes are 355 to 383 ci. For this book, we built a 355-ci engine that is almost as powerful as a 383-ci version, for a lot less money.

Prepping for Assembly

The only LT block options are whether you have two- or four-bolt main bearing caps. Otherwise, the blocks are the same. When starting to plan your project, try your best to get steel caps and straps, have the deck heights checked and corrected, and ensure the lifter bores are all measured (once in awhile you find one that is scuffed up).

The block must be cleaned before you begin. We use a method that bakes the block like cleaning an oven, and then it is shot blasted. Now it is ready to be checked for any cracks. If we are going to overbore the cylinders more than .030-inch, we sonic-check all the cylinder bores for wall thickness. The LT block easily goes .060-inch oversize for a normally aspirated application. We have built several LT-based engines at 4.100 inches (.100-inch oversize). In fact, my (Myron's) personal 1954 Chevy Sedan Delivery is powered by a 409-ci 548-hp LT1 with a 4.100-inch bore. Something to keep in mind is that the thinner the walls are, the harder it is to keep cool.

Installing crankshaft to check deck height.

ASSEMBLY

Line boring the mains.

Main Bearing Caps and Straps

Once the walls pass inspection, we tap the threads on all of the bolt holes in the block. Any damaged or stripped bolt holes are repaired. The block is now ready to have the main bearing caps and straps installed. You need to find the best-possible machine shop to do this work, where the technicians are familiar with the intricacies of this operation. When the angled (splayed) bolt holes are drilled, it is important that they do not go into the water jacket, which would lead to a coolant leak that would be difficult to locate. Another item that is often overlooked is the dipstick clearance near the fourth main bearing cap.

The block should now be ready to have the newly installed caps and straps align bored, leaving some material for finish align honing.

Crankshaft

After a thorough cleaning, a Magnaflux inspection (for cracks), and a dimensional check, you have some options. If it is a very nice crankshaft, you can balance it and give it a polish on the machined surfaces. This includes de-burring and a good brushing of the oil holes. You may choose to have the crankshaft ground; if you do, be sure to specify the final journal size.

One option with factory cast or steel shafts is to have them nitride coated. This is a surface hardness treatment that helps a crankshaft last linger and survive in harsh environments. The first step is to have the shaft normalized, which makes it stable so that after grinding (when it goes to the heat treater) it needs only a minimum amount of straightening. The result is a crankshaft with a very hard surface that is scuff resistant. This is not cheap, but as a rule it is less expensive than a new aftermarket crankshaft. Of course if you are building a stroker with a new (longer stroke) crankshaft, you do not have do this.

Another option is to cryogenically treat the parts. This has been popular with top-of-the-line builders with good results. This ultra-cold treatment aligns the molecular structure in the metal, resulting in a stronger part.

Pistons

The next piece of the short-block puzzle is the pistons and wrist pin assembly. Custom pistons vary in quality. The most important dimension is the piston-to-wall clearance. The most critical surface is the bottom of the ring lands, because if the ring grooves are not ultra-smooth, combustion gases can blow under the ring and cause a large loss of power. That also means that the ring end gaps need to be set precisely.

The wrist-pin-to-piston clearance is usually set by the manufacturer, but it still needs to be checked. If it is too tight, it scuffs. If it is too loose, you hear a little noise that is a "double chuckle" under a no-load situation. For a mild street engine, something about .0005-inch is in order. A maximum-effort drag racing engine commands .0009-inch clearance.

The piston rings are next. Again, all of the dimensions need to be checked. This includes groove depth and width and of course, the end gap when the bores are finished.

At this point we bore the block giving the pistons just enough clearance so that after a quick hone and run through the hot tank we can mock up the assembly. The reason for not finishing the bore at this time is to keep the piston stable in the bore, which makes an accurate deck-height check possible.

We've chosen to use a full-floating-design piston pin in this engine. These require no special preparation techniques and make assembly relatively easy. If you have a press-fit pin setup, you need to make a test pin out of aluminum to avoid ruining (and buying!) the wrong piston.

To check the deck height, put a piston and rod assembly in the four corner bores and measure the amount that needs to be cut. Today's engine blocks are much better when it comes to the factory machine work. The target dimension is around .002 inch, end-to-end. For all cast-iron blocks with steel connecting rods, set the deck height at zero and use a .040-inch-thick head gasket. This gives a quench clearance that promotes a quick mixture motion, leading to a chamber that is not as octane sensitive. Also look up at the pin end to make sure that the small end of the rod has clearance in the piston. Once you're satisfied that the reciprocating assembly has proper clearances throughout, run everything through the hot tank again.

Next, check for piston-to-valve clearance (we assume the heads are assembled and ready to go). Remove the springs from the number-1 cylinder and substitute a set of lightweight springs to make the job of checking easier. We use a set of old cam bearings that had the OD turned down so that they just slip in. Remember, we are going to go back to the hone to finish the bores and a final cleaning so we don't want to drive in a new set of cam bearings only to take them out again.

The piston-to-valve clearance needs to be sufficient so the valves and pistons never make contact. There are several things to consider: whether you'll be using an automatic or manual gearbox, whether the engine will be living on the street or the dragstrip, or both, etc. All of these factors have a bearing on your decisions regarding the finishing details. Let's assume everything is average for this particular build.

The intake valve clearance is usually less than the exhaust valve clearance. The reason for this is that the piston chases the exhaust valve up the bore on the exhaust stroke. If you are at the limit of the valvetrain's ability to control the valve motion, things begin to crash. Conversely, the intake valve chases the piston down the bore, and this puts the intake components under compression. Therefore, less clearance is needed. A good number for the exhaust is .100 to .125 inch, and the intake only needs .060 to .080 inch.

At this time you should check the compression ratio to make sure that it meets your specification. You need a dab of oil on the top ring on the piston to help seal things up. We use a Katech Whistler tool to accomplish this, but you could use a CC tube to figure out the compression ratio the old-fashioned way—by measuring the volume of the bore, gasket, and cylinder head at both bottom dead center (BDC) and top dead center (TDC) and comparing them to create a ratio.

Bore Honing

The short block is now ready for the bores to be honed to their final size. The piston-to-wall clearance that you end up with depends on the piston alloy. The block is run through

To install the cam bearings, start at the rear and work forward. Make sure the oil feed holes are facing the crankshaft. All cam bearings face the crankshaft. This becomes obvious when you see the main caps with the oil feed hole facing you.

ASSEMBLY

the hot tank for the final time, paying the most attention to the bores. Before using a compressed-air blowgun, wipe the block with a clean white cloth coated with a rust preventative, such as AMSOIL MP. This keeps a rust haze from forming in the bores and is also the only thing that we are going to use on the bores themselves during final assembly.

Ring Gap

Next, the ring end gap needs to be checked with a feeler gauge and corrected. This can be done with a file or with a specialty ring grinder. Follow the piston and ring manufacturer's gap recommendation. With too little clearance, you take a big chance of pulling a ring land off when the engine gets up to temperature. With too much ring gap, you have excessive blow-by, oil burning, and lots of smoke out the exhaust pipe. The proper gap is critical, so take the time to ensure it's right.

Piston Pin Locks

Begin final assembly with the installation of the piston pin locks. Once you have one set of locks in the pistons, add a drop of oil in the pin bores. Install the pin in the piston and move the pin in and out to make sure the oil is spread evenly. Wipe a little oil in the small end of the rod. Hook the two together and install the remaining pin locks. The end play of the wrist pin needs to be near zero. Otherwise the pin can act as a battering ram and drive the locks out.

Plugs

With the pistons hung on the rods and ready to install, you can prepare the block for them. Install all the galley and frost plugs.

Next come the cam bearings, and then install the camshaft and make sure it turns freely.

Main Bearing Clearance Measurement

Install a main bearing and torque the cap. Measure the vertical clearance. We like to set the clearance between .0018 and .0020 inch. This applies to most engines. Any more than this makes the rotating assembly flow too much oil, resulting in oil pressure problems, such as low oil pressure at a hot idle. We use the same clearance on the rod bearings.

One note here is that some crankshafts have very large radii filets. Be sure that the bearings do touch in this area; this means the rod bearings also.

Inspect Oil Galley Plugs

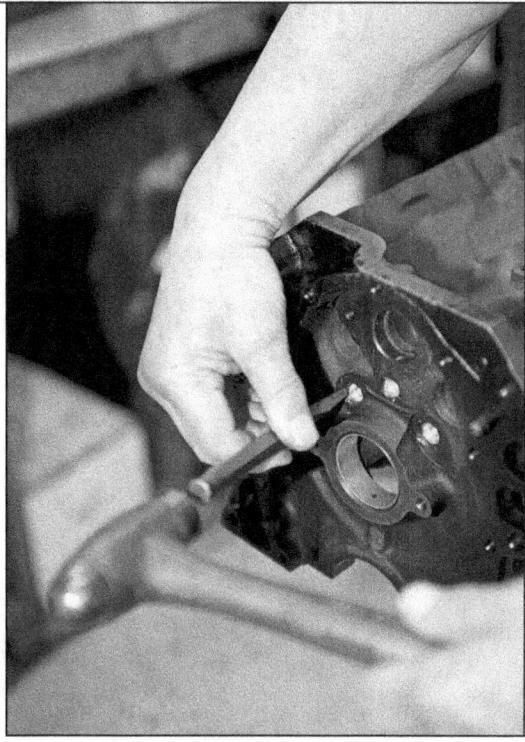

1 *The galley plugs here are the factory style, pressed in and then staked with a chisel. This motor is mild-performance, so factory plugs are just fine.*

Inspect Oil Galley Plugs (Continued)

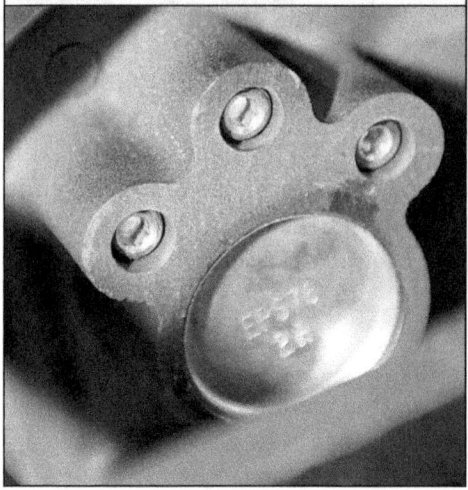

2 There is an important galley plug at the rear of the engine not to miss. If you do, oil squirts all over the place, requiring you to remove the head and install the plug.

Note Drive Type

3 The rear plugs are screw-in types. Notice the Allen-key-style drive.

Choose Lube

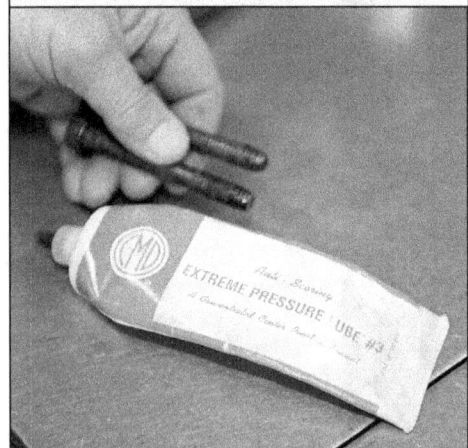

4 We swear by this type of lube for our assemblies.

5 Use the lube on the threads and under the head of the bolts; tighten to 70 ft-lbs of torque.

Tighten Bolts

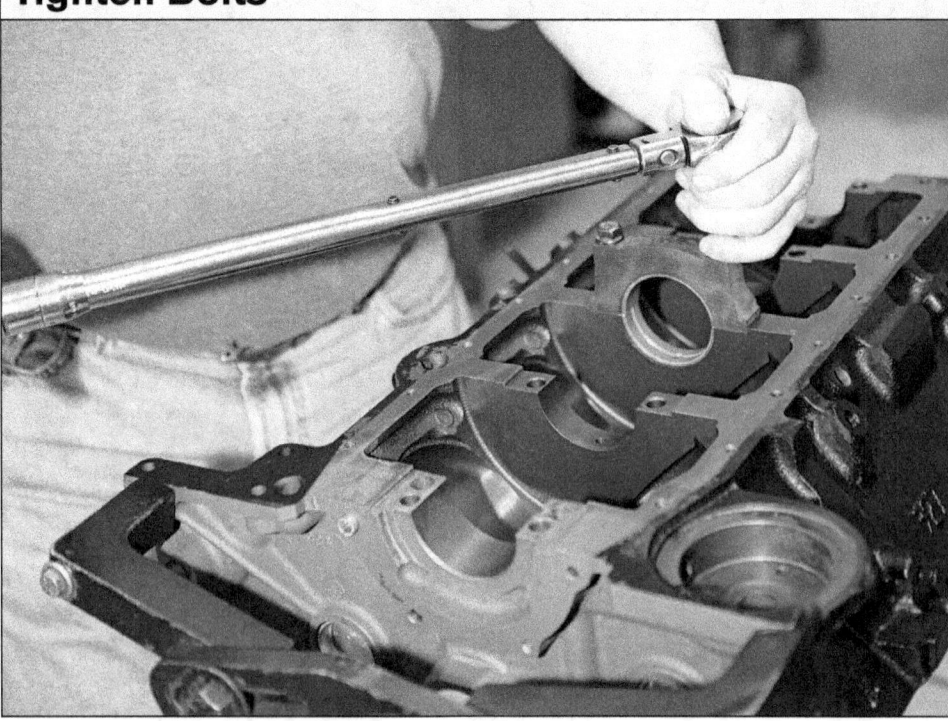

ASSEMBLY

Measure Clearance

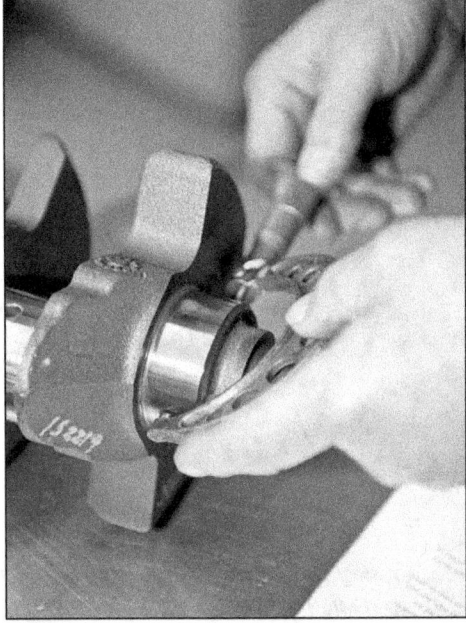

6 The correct way to measure rod or main bearing clearance is to use an inside and outside micrometer. Although it's common practice to use Plasti-gauge, we feel that the micrometer is far more accurate.

7 This is a very delicate operation and requires "feel." If you are ham-fisted, try not to do this on your own. For this build we had a clearance of .0018 inch, which is what we want for a solid build. We want it below .002 and over .0018 inch of clearance.

Lube Bearings

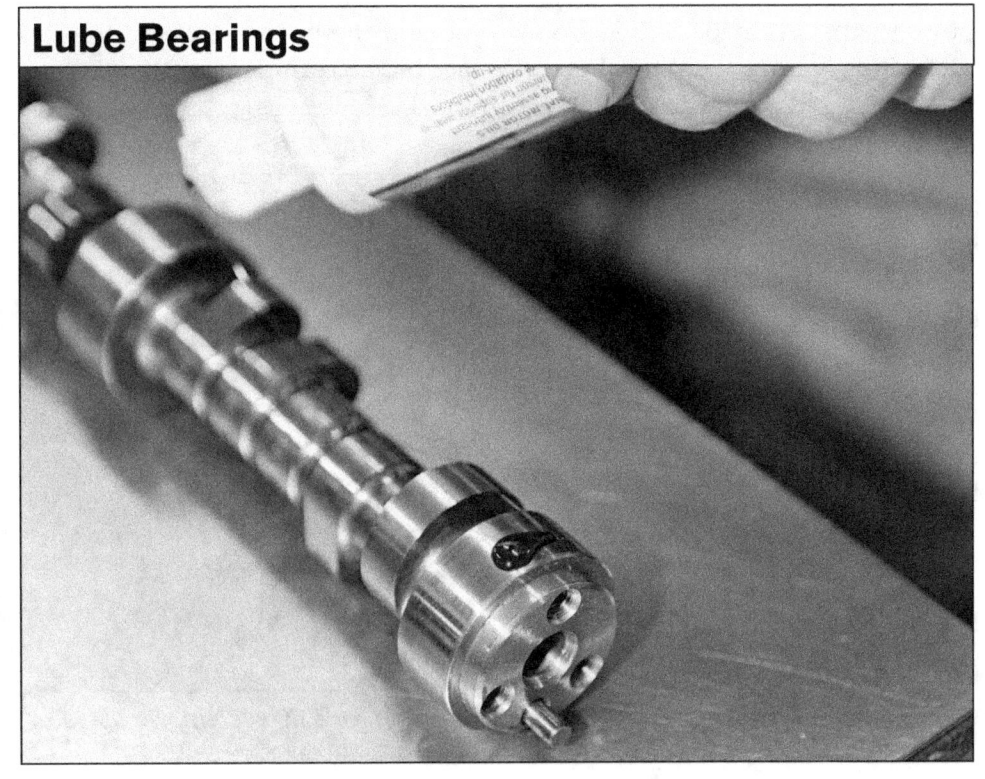

Choose Break-in Lube

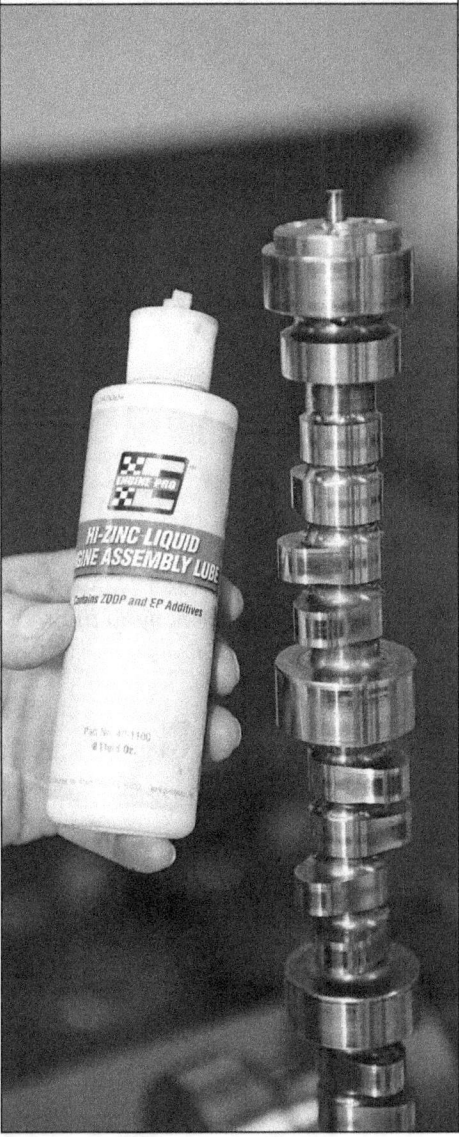

8 It is very important that you use a break-in lube with high zinc content, so the zinc acts as a barrier between the metals.

9 A small dab of lubricant on each bearing should do the trick.

HOW TO BUILD MAX-PERFORMANCE CHEVY LT1/LT4 ENGINES   89

Check Galley Plug

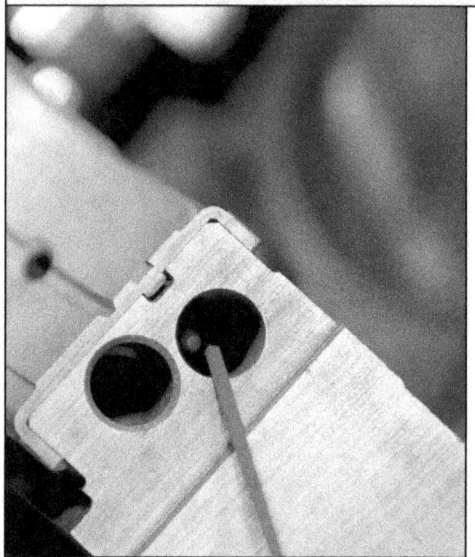  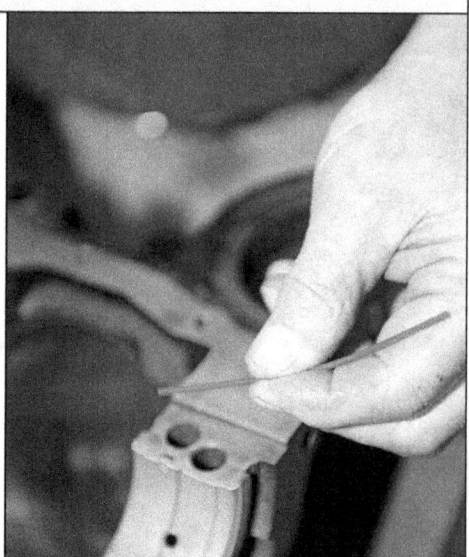

10 This series of photos shows the hidden galley plug that is inside the marked hole. Without this, the oil travels from the oil pump directly to the bearing, essentially bypassing the oil filter. This will cost you a motor! Triple check that this plug has been installed.

Bore Preparation

All the piston and rod assemblies are ready to be installed.

To prepare the bores, wipe each bore briskly with a clean rag soaked in some lacquer thinner until the rag comes out clean. Then coat the bores with Amsoil MP, leaving a light film.

Next, put a small amount of Total-Seal (a quick-seal dry assembly lube) on your finger. This is a black powder that provides the proper lubrication during the critical break-in period. It virtually eliminates cylinder-wall burnishing and glazing. Rub the top 2 inches of the bore with your finger. If you have done a good job and the bores are clean, the surface has a greenish cast to it.

Inspect Machine

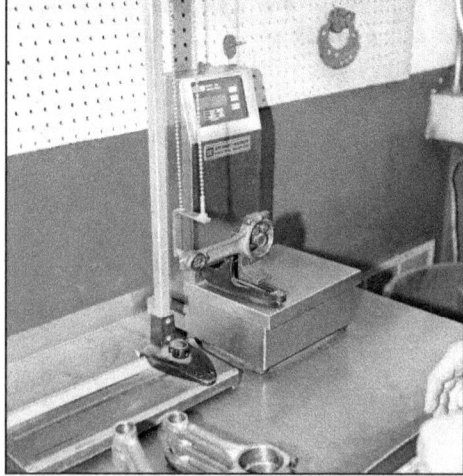

1 This scale and fixture is used for determining the big-end weight of the connecting rod.

Use Belt Sander

2 To get all the end weights of the connecting rods consistent, we use a belt sander.

ASSEMBLY

Create Balance Sheet

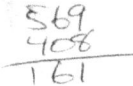
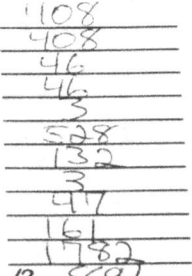

Weight of Crank End of Connecting Rod — 408
Weight of Crank End of Connecting Rod — 408
Weight of Set of Bearings — 46
Weight of Set of Bearings — 46
Weight of Oil (Estimated) — 5
Weight of Piston — 528
Weight of Piston Pin — 132
Weight of Piston Pin Locks — 3
Weight of One Set of Piston Rings — 47
Weight of Piston End of Connecting Rod — 161
Bobweight Total — 1782 /2 — 891

3 All the rods are weighed to find the lightest. The other seven are then machined to make them all weigh the same. The rest of the components of the connecting rod assembly are also weighed as a unit. Notice on the balance sheet that we use two big ends as part of the calculation because there are two big ends on each crank journal along with two sets of rod bearings. For the rest of the components, we use one of each and then 5 grams for oil. Add the column and divide by 2. Each number is now half of the bob-weight.

Disassemble Bob-weight

4 Here's how a bob-weight comes apart. Great care must be taken installing them to get them evenly spaced across each journal. (The crank is then spun to determine the crank balance throughout the RPM range.)

HOW TO BUILD MAX-PERFORMANCE CHEVY LT1/LT4 ENGINES

Tighten or Loosen Connecting Rod Bolts

5 *The wrong way (top left); the "just OK" way (top right) to loosen rod bolts. This (bottom left and bottom right) is the correct way to loosen them.*

ASSEMBLY

Measure Rod Bearing Clearance

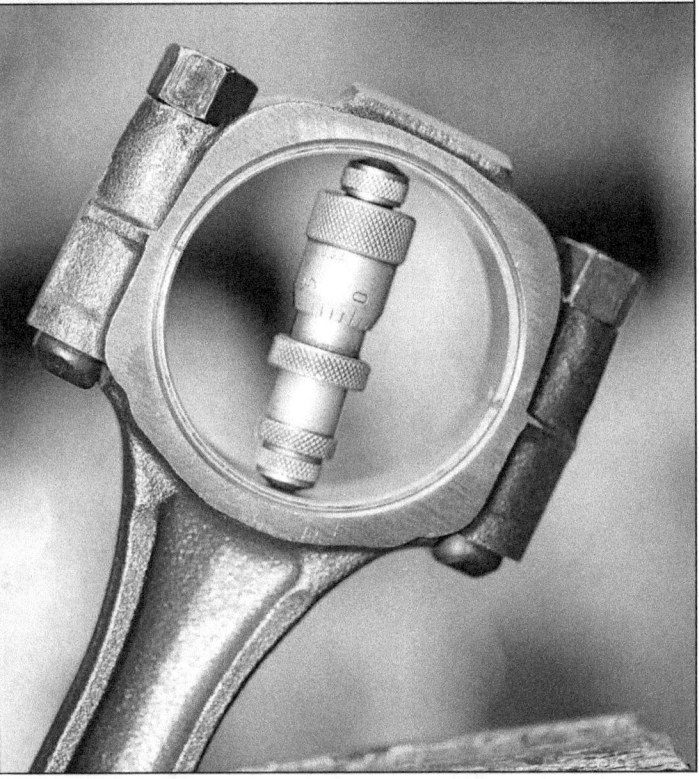

6 The correct way to measure rod bearing clearance is to use an inside and outside micrometer.

Insert Ring into Bore

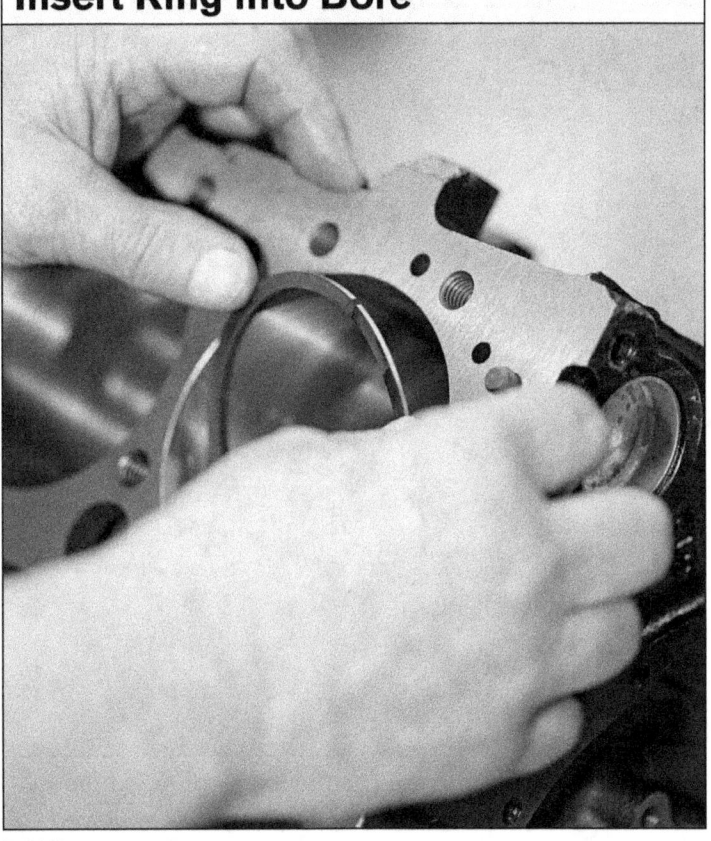

7 Tip the ring into the bore carefully.

Square Ring

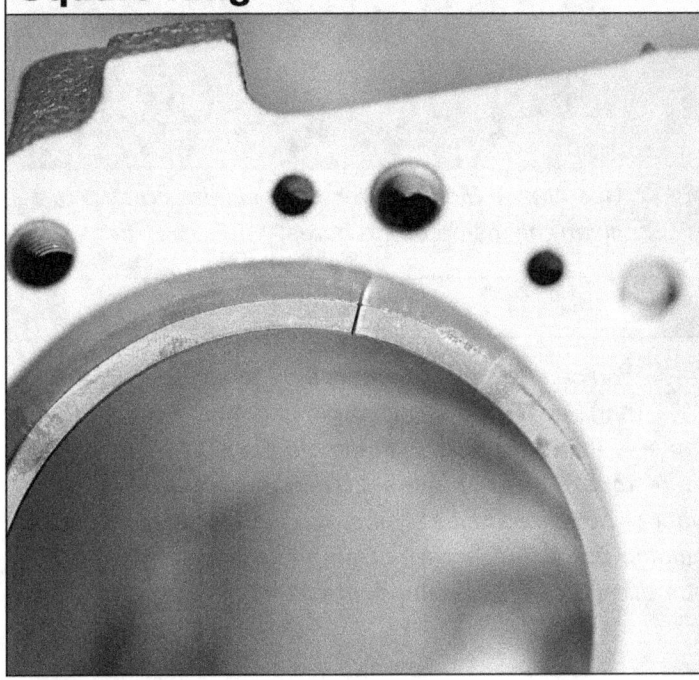

8 Use ring-squaring tool to level the ring inside the cylinder bore.

Measure End Gap

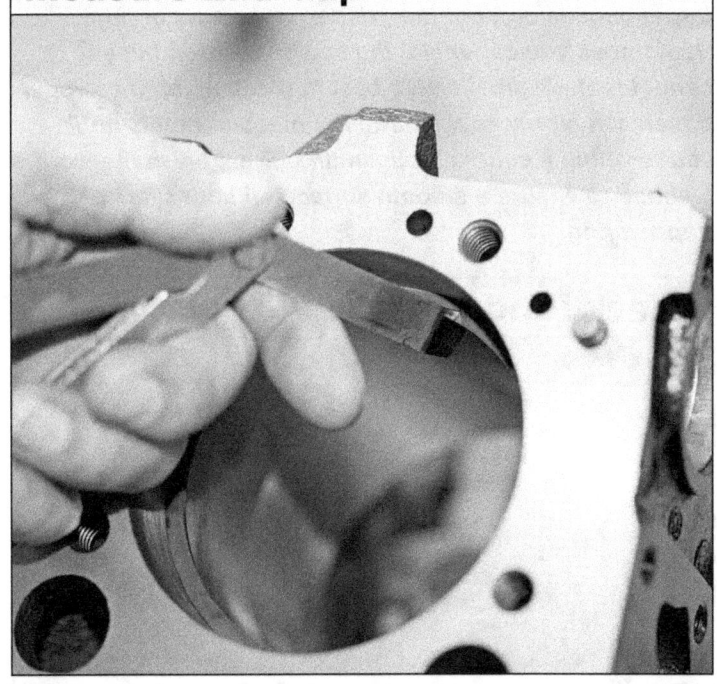

9 Use feeler gauge to measure end gap. Minimum end gap is 4.5 x bore diameter in thousands of an inch.

HOW TO BUILD MAX-PERFORMANCE CHEVY LT1/LT4 ENGINES

Adjust End Gap

10 Piston ring end gap is adjusted by grinding the ends of the ring until the proper gap is achieved. The proper way to do this is by using a piston ring grinder (shown). It can also be done by hand filing (which should still be done after the ring is gapped very close to the target dimension), but the grinder saves a lot of time. Remember, you can make the end gap larger, but you cannot make it smaller. It's best to creep up on the proper dimension slowly, making regular measurements until you're within a couple thousandths. Then, finish the work by hand to ensure a smooth surface on both sides of the gapped ring.

Clean Inside of Bore

11 Use Amsoil Metal Protector or similar product to clean the inside of the bores.

Check Ring Seat

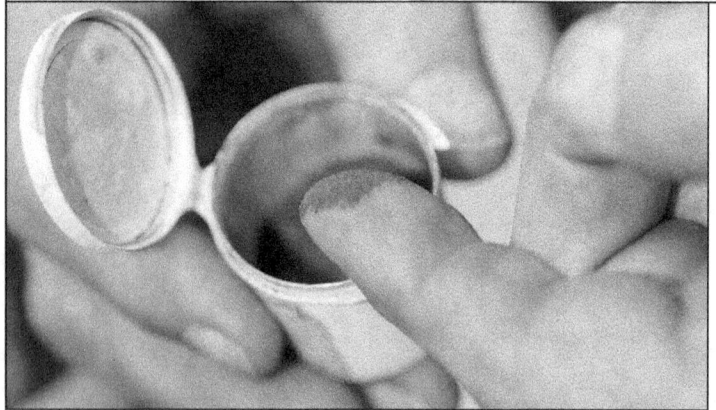

12 You can use dry assembly lube to ensure that the rings seat properly. Doing this gets a much faster ring seal than ever before. In the old days, builders dunked the pistons in oil prior to installation. Today's modern cylinder bores are miles ahead of previous years of engine building due to modern machining tolerances. When the lube turns green, it is done doing its job.

ASSEMBLY

Bottom End Assembly

Once you've accomplished all of the prep work, you can begin the bottom end assembly process. The actual assembly process doesn't take nearly as much time as the preparation. Knowing everything will fit correctly and that all of the bearing clearances are correct means you can simply put the parts together. Remember to use a quality assembly lubricant on all of the bearing surfaces prior to assembly.

Crankshaft Installation

Once you are happy with the clearance on the main bearings, it's time to install the crankshaft. For years we have used Amsoil synthetic gear lube as the assembly oil. We use it everywhere. You don't need much. Our rule is that if it drips on the floor, you have used too much.

There's no real trick here; just be careful, as you need to make sure that you have proper end play, and that the rear of the thrust face on the center main is seated against the thrust surface on the crankshaft.

Choose Gear Lube

1 We use Amsoil gear lube to assemble the motor.

Align Bearing Tangs

2 Align the tangs of the bearings together for proper alignment. Make sure the back of the bearing is completely dry before installing.

Prepare to Torque Bolts

3 Running the bolts down saves time before torquing them.

Torque Bolts

4 Spin the crank as you torque down the main caps to check for freedom. Start torquing the caps at 45 ft-lbs and then proceed to the final torque rating of 70 ft-lbs.

Align Crankshaft Thrust Surfaces

5 Force the crankshaft forward (as shown with a screwdriver between the main cap and the crankshaft, arrow) and gently tap the rear cap to the rear. When completed, set up your dial indicator and determine crankshaft endplay. You should have approximately .003 to .005 inch. The crankshaft must turn freely with no sticking points.

ASSEMBLY

Piston and Rod Assembly Installation

You are now ready to install the piston and rod assemblies. We use very little lube because when an engine runs there is very little oil above the ring travel.

In the old days, dipping the piston in a can of oil was overkill. We put just a drop of oil on the skirt of the piston and rub it around, and make no attempt to lube the rings; that job is for the Quick Seat lube powder.

Install your tapered-ring compressor over the rings, being sure to space the ring end gaps evenly. Put a spot of oil on the rod bearing and install. At this time do not torque the rod bolts, just snug them. When you have all eight pistons installed, torque the rod bolts. Once this is done, be sure to move each rod pair back and forth to make certain that the rod seats against the crank cheek. Some of today's aftermarket crankshafts have extra-large radii filets, which causes an interference between the edge of the rod or main bearing and the filet. Also many of today's rod bearings have a top and a bottom.

Lubricate Piston

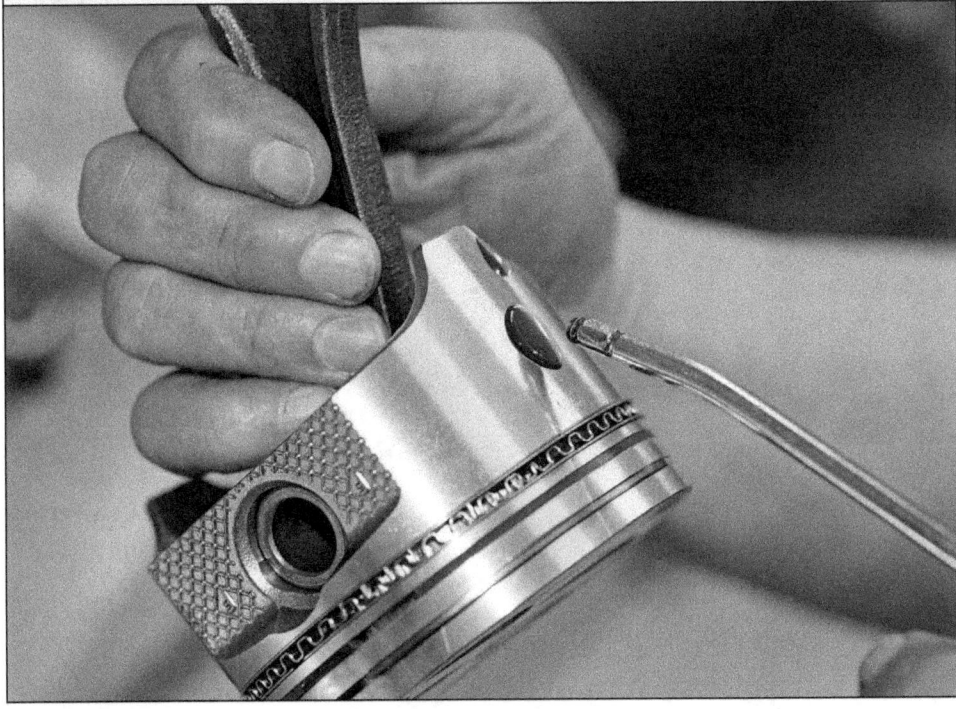

1 *A small dab of oil should do the trick to make sure the piston is lubricated properly while you run it home.*

Check for Interference

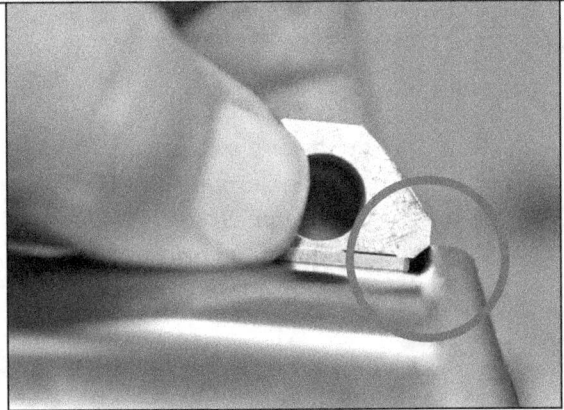

2 *Under certain circumstances, some components may have interference between the crank journal and the rod bearing (left). If this is the case in your build, you must chamfer the bearings to avoid rubbing (right).*

Install Oil Rings

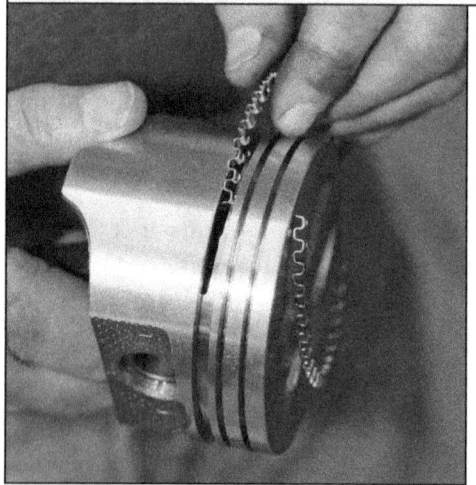 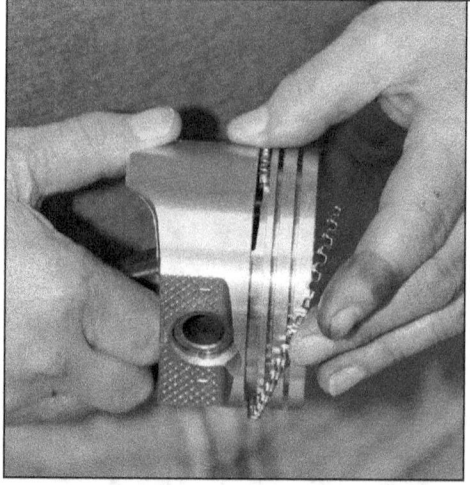 

3 Install the oil ring in its groove. We use a method of rolling it into place rather than spreading it. This is the same for the top and bottom rings.

Check Skirt Diameter

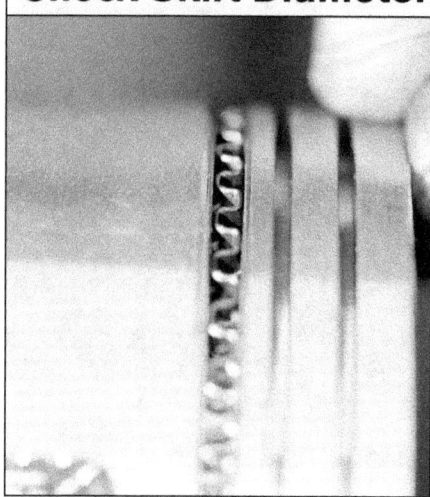

4 Make sure that all rings go below the surface of the piston. The skirt diameter of the piston is wider by approximately .020 inch than the top lands of the piston. It is therefore important that the rings do not protrude beyond the surface.

Use Alignment Marks

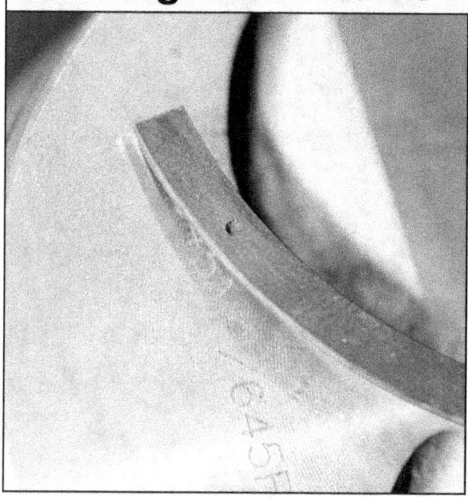

5 If the rings are marked, the marks must face upward. All ring packages come with instructions, make sure to follow the specific instructions for your set.

Install Top and Second Ring

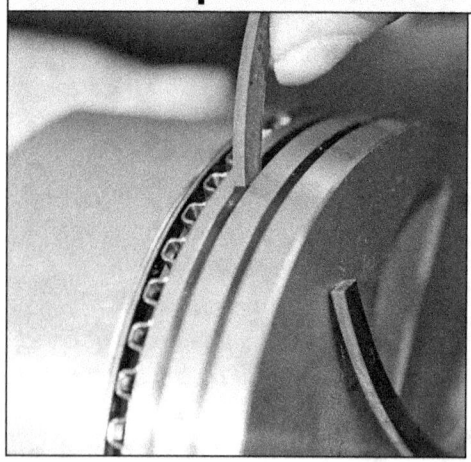

6 Install the top and second ring by inserting the tip gently and sliding the rings around the piston. Offset the ring gaps prior to installation.

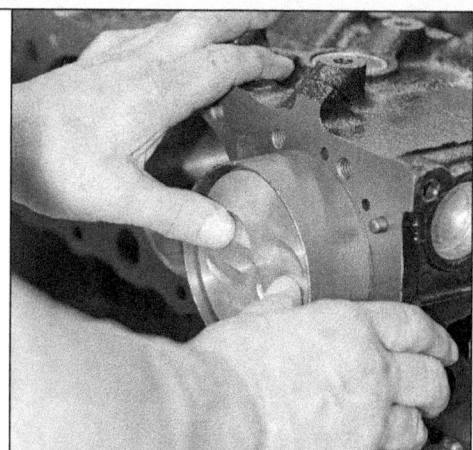

7 If the ring package tension is light you may be able to push the piston in with your hands.

ASSEMBLY

Tap Ring into Place

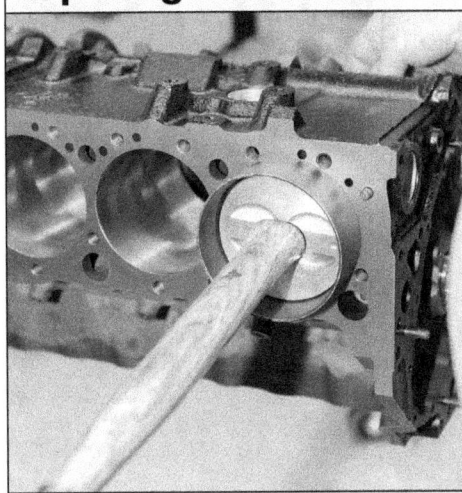

8 Stiffer-tension ring packages may need to be rammed home with the butt end of a hammer.

Guide Connecting Rod

9 Guiding the connecting rod onto the crank ensures it does not knick the crank journal. There is a tool for this, but after forty years I use my fingers.

Check Clearance Between Piston and Connecting Rod Small End

10 Make sure that you have enough clearance between the two when installing your pistons. We have seen instances where custom rods, custom pistons, and custom crank shafts incur binding issues that can lead to catastrophic failure of the motor.

Install Camshaft

11 Installing the camshaft requires a steady hand, as not to damage or mar the soft cam bearing surfaces.

Install Water Pump Drive

12 Gently tap the water pump drive into place, being careful not to hit the sprockets, as they could gall.

Add Loctite to Threads

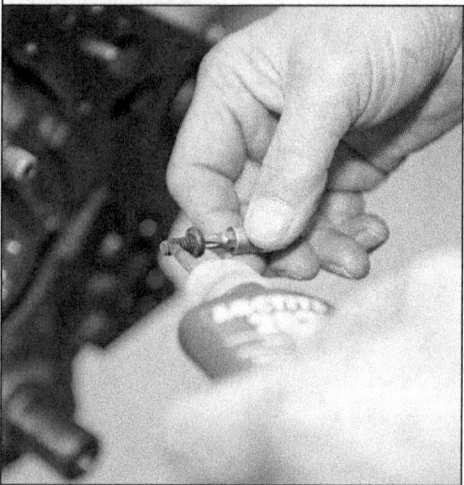

13 A dab of Red Loctite on the threads is plenty to keep the retaining bolts in place.

Spin Bearing

14 Spin the bearing to make sure it is free and does not hang up.

Add Loctite to Cam Retainers

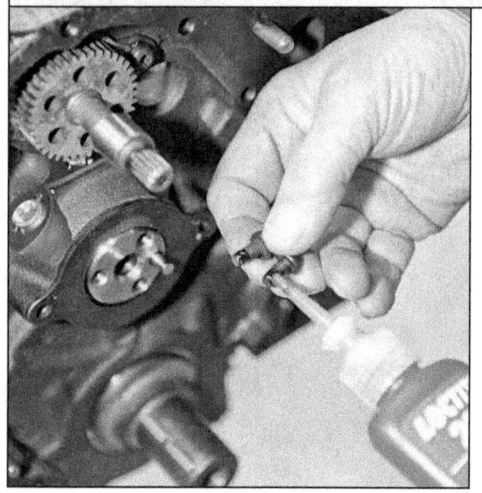

15 Another dab of Loctite goes on the cam retainers.

Install Camshaft Thrust Plate

16 Cam retainer and fasteners are installed using Loctite.

ASSEMBLY

TDC and Timing Verification

The LT1 does not have a TDC pointer, which is not important if you are using the factory ECUs. But if you are using an aftermarket system such as MoTeC, or FAST, you want to have the ability to check the timing. These systems have a feature that allows you to adjust the timing offset so that TDC on your laptop agrees with your timing light. To do this, you have to put the crankshaft at TDC and create a timing mark. The hub does not have a keyway, so you have to machine one.

You need this TDC mark to begin the process of degreeing in the camshaft.

For the purpose of verifying ignition timing with a computer-controlled ECU, you need to have a TDC reference. To do that you must key the hub to the crank so that it is installed the same way each time. Once the hub and dampener are installed, make a reference mark on the distributor and dampner. Use a dial indicator to find TDC, as shown.

Timing Chain and Cover, Optispark and Rear Seal Installation

It is now time to install the front cover with the Optispark along with the damper and water pump.

The rear seal is next. It is important to note that some seals on the engine are installed dry and others need to be oiled. Read the instructions that come with the seals.

Align Cam Gear Dot

1 *When installing the Cloyes timing set, make sure to align the cam gear dot with the crank gear's round marking, which can be difficult to see. This is for the factory-specified timing. To advance the timing, use the triangle marking and the square marking to retard the timing, per the instructions.*

HOW TO BUILD MAX-PERFORMANCE CHEVY LT1/LT4 ENGINES

CHAPTER 7

Degreeing the Camshaft

All camshafts should be degreed upon installation. While this procedure is not difficult, you will need a few simple tools including a degree wheel and a dial indicator.

The first step is to bring the number-1 piston to TDC and install your degree wheel and pointer, setting the wheel to zero. Next, set up your dial indicator on the lifter tappet and set the lash to zero. The first check is to find TDC of the intake centerline. If the cam is to be installed at 105 degrees, when you rotate the crankshaft until the indicator is at maximum lobe lift, the pointer should be aiming at 105 on the degree wheel.

Next, zero your indicator. I like to take all measurements in the direction that the motor rotates. (The cams that we use have asymmetrical lobes, meaning that the opening side of lobe has a different geometric shape than the closing side.) Now you pick the amount that you are going to use for your averaging; I use .020 inch.

The assembly is still sitting on your 105-degree point. To begin the process of confirming that, rotate the assembly counterclockwise until your dial indicator drops about .050 inch. Then, rotate the engine clockwise until you approach .020 inch on your dial indicator. Mark your degree wheel at the pointer, and then continue to rotate the assembly past the dial indicator zero and on to .020 inch past the peak lift point. Again, mark your degree wheel at the pointer. The exact distance between the two marks on the degree wheel is your lobe centerline. Put a mark on your wheel and count back from zero to your mark—this is your intake centerline. If this is not within the specifications called out on the cam card, move the cam (typically accomplished by using offset bushings on the pin in the cam gear, or through the use of the alternate keyways in the crank gear) and redo the test until it is.

Assembled timing chain and water pump drive. This version is installed with the late-style heavy-duty LT4 chain and gear set.

Install Crank Gear

2 *Use solid blows to install the crank gear; this may take a few jolts to get it seated properly.*

Install Cam Gear

3 *Set the motor to TDC and install the cam gear with the chain. Again, Loctite is your friend with the retaining bolts.*

ASSEMBLY

Tighten Camshaft Retaining Bolts

4 Tighten camshaft retaining bolts to 30 ft-lbs.

Install Reluctor Wheel

5 Install the reluctor wheel, keyed properly.

Apply Lube to Seals

6 Prior to installing the seals, it is always a good idea to apply a thin coat of lubricant such as grease on the sealing lip and shaft per the instructions from Fel-Pro. Press these seals in with a large socket or a flat plate and a hammer. In this case, we use a press, which is ultimately the correct way. Be sure to put solid support under the cover to ensure that you do not scratch or mar the polished cover.

HOW TO BUILD MAX-PERFORMANCE CHEVY LT1/LT4 ENGINES

CHAPTER 7

Apply RTV to Cover Gasket

7 Apply a thin layer of RTV to hold the cover gasket in place.

Apply RTV to Cover

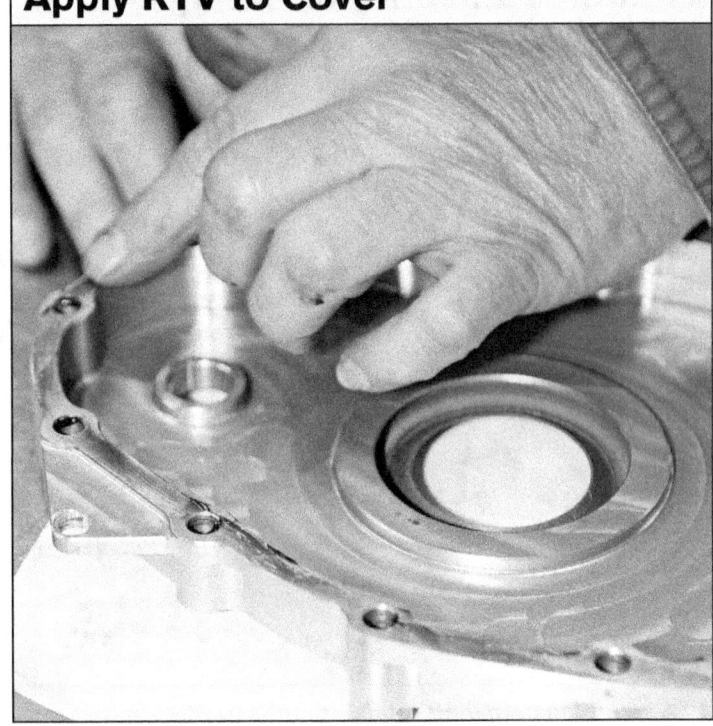

8 Repeat the process on the cover.

Tap on Timing Cover

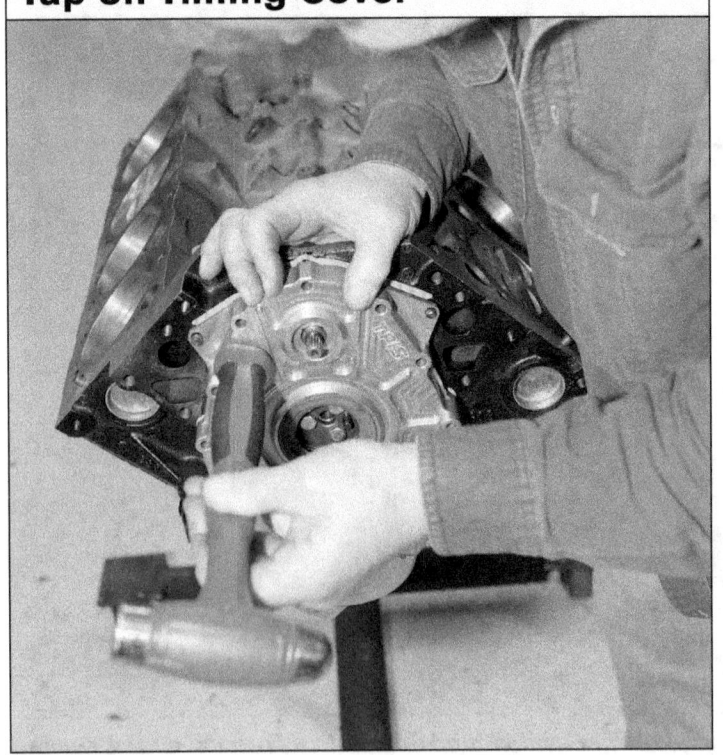

9 The timing cover may require some persuasion from a rubber mallet or, in our case, the plastic butt end of a hammer.

Choose Timing Cover Bolts

10 There are two lengths of bolts for the timing cover; finding the correct ones should be fairly straightforward.

Install Distributor Shaft Seal

11 The distributor shaft seal is a PTFE seal and must be installed dry. Do not lubricate the lip or the seal. Put this seal in when the cover is installed on the motor. Caution: The seal tends to fold over itself and cause a lot of headaches for owners when the seal leaks.

12 The best way to ensure that the seal does not leak is to work inward toward the gear prior to installation so that it does not hang up. We use a spare gear set to massage it into shape. You are not able to see if it is hung up until you start the motor.

Verify Crank Timing

13 We cut a keyway into the crank hub to verify that the crank is properly timed and to verify the accuracy of the timing. You may need to have a machine shop complete this task for you.

Align Distributor to Camshaft

14 Ultimately, it may be easier to remove the cover of the distributor to align it to the camshaft. The size for this is an E4 Torx bit.

Install Hub

15 Pound the hub into place until it seats flush against the timing gear.

Add Lube to Rear Seal

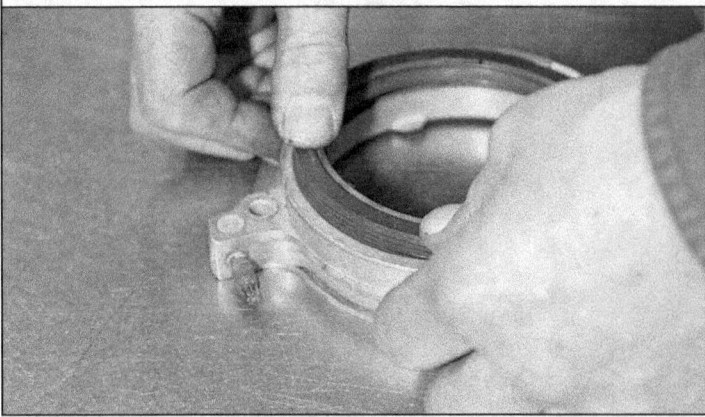

16 *The rear seal gets a small amount of assembly lube to help drive it home and seal it well.*

Find Gasket Stud

17 *The rear main seal adapter gasket on the driver's side should have a stud. The passenger side has an indexing dowel.*

Install Rear Main Seal

18 *Installing the rear main seal requires care so as to not let the seal fold upon itself. Do not use a screwdriver to do this; use your finger to massage it onto the crank, working it back and forth until it seats.*

Oil System and Pan Installation

More often than not we find there is too much oil pressure when setting up the oil pump. The old rule of having 10 pounds for each 1,000 rpm is okay up 5,000 rpm. After that, it gets to be too much. My (Myron) World Challenge competition Camaro was about 40 psi at 7,000 rpm. After two years of racing, the bearings looked like new.) The spring that comes in a standard oil pump is usually set to bypass at about 40 psi with hot oil. This should be enough. You might shim the spring with one washer.

The next thing is to set the clearance between the bottom of the pickup and the pan. This dimension should be 1/4 to 3/8 inch. As for the oil pan, we typically use a road-race style as most of our customers run F- and Y-Body cars.

Inspect Valley Pan Spider Spring

1 Here, the valley pan spider spring is resting in position.

Install Oil Pump Pickup

2 Installing the oil pump pick up often requires a special tool and often requires welding to keep it in place.

Test Fit Oil Pan

3 Using a piece of clay and some plastic, we place the oil pan over the pump to get a satisfactory distance between the pump and pan. The ideal depth is 3/8 inch.

Pre-Lube Oil Pump

4 Pre-lubing the oil pump helps it prime faster. You must prime the pump before you start the engine for the first time.

ASSEMBLY

Add RTV to Oil Pan Gasket

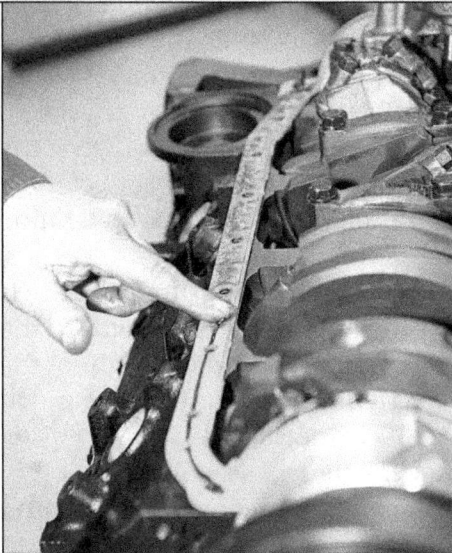

5 *A good bead of RTV on both sides of the Fel-Pro one-piece oil pan gasket is needed.*

Install Oil Pan

6 *The bottom is capped off by the oil pan. (In this photo you can see that the cylinder heads are already in place. You can install the oil pan before you install the heads.)*

Add Oil Pan Straps

7 *Straps are added to make sure the oil pan has been evenly snugged into place. They should be tightened until compression is made on the gasket. We let the RTV set for 24 hours and then come back to retighten the bolts.*

CHAPTER 7

Top End Assembly

Installing the heads is pretty straightforward. There are just a few things to think about. We typically use new head bolts; it is cheaper than cleaning the old ones. As for head studs we do not use them on blocks with bolt holes that go into water. They almost always weep coolant into the crankcase or dribble down the outside of the engine. We use CMD Extreme Pressure Lube Number 3 under the head of the bolt. On the threads, we use silicone sealant or a Teflon sealant. The heads are torqued in the normal fashion in accordance with the factory circular torque pattern.

On new aluminum heads, we use a brass drift and a large hammer to give each bolt a medium rap after the initial torque. Then, we loosen each bolt and re-torque. The aluminum compresses and work-hardens. This technique allows the bolts to remain at the proper torque setting.

When installing the valvetrain, it is important to make sure that the rocker arm geometry is correct. One of the major factors that determine the correct geometry is the length of the pushrods. Pushrod length is directly affected by the length of the tappet and the installed height of the valvestem, and needs to be measured carefully prior to assembly to ensure proper length

Once the geometry is set and the valves are adjusted, it is time to prime the oil pump. This needs to be done before the stock LT1 intake is installed, because there is no provision on the intake to use the traditional oil pump priming tool. Be sure to install the oil filter, plug the oil pressure port, and that the drain plug is tight with a new gasket. Put in your oil of choice. Once you have primed the pump install the oil pump drive before installing the intake.

Next, install the intake manifold. Start by doing a test fit without any sealant. Use the gaskets that match your port size; the LT has little plastic dowels that hold the gaskets in place. There should be around .040-inch clearances under both ends of the manifold, as this allows the manifold to settle. Check for both bolt hole alignment and intake port alignment. Once you are satisfied, put a little silicone around the water ports and the bottom of the intake ports along with a bead at each end of the block. Set the intake manifold in place and just snug the bolts. We are going to come back in a few hours and finish tightening the bolts to the specified torque.

Head Installation

Choose Gaskets

1 *We are using Victor Reinz gaskets (PN 5898). We did not deck this block, resulting in a .030-inch deck height. To compensate we use a .030-inch-thick head gasket, which gives a quench clearance of .060 inch, which is .020 inch more than what is considered ideal.*

Add Thread Sealer

2 *A small dab of Teflon thread sealer on each thread helps seal the holes from water.*

ASSEMBLY

Tighten Head Bolts

3 Head bolts are tightened in three equal steps to 70 ft-lbs with a dose of fastener assembly lube. In the approved sequence, bolts are tightened in a circular pattern. The first lap starts at 30 ft-lbs, the second lap at 50 ft-lbs, and the third onto 70 ft-lbs. A smooth, careful motion with a quality torque wrench is your best bet.

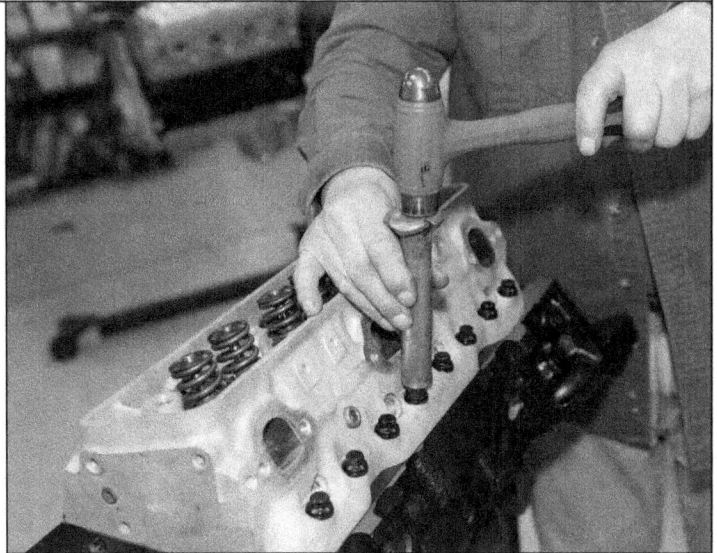

4 A couple firm taps on each head bolt and then another round of tightening to 70 ft-lbs saves you a lot of work later when retorquing the heads. This works best on new heads and less so on older used heads. This may seem a little crude, but it is quite effective and saves a retorque later.

Valvetrain Installation

Add Lube to Lifters

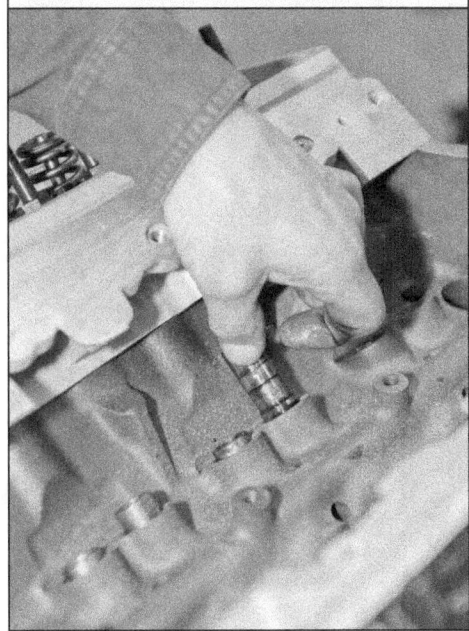

1 With a liberal amount of zinc-laden assembly lube, the lifters come next.

Inspect Tie Bars

2 These tie bars have the flat end matching the flat end of the lifter. Tie bars are essential and must not be omitted.

Add Lube to Pushrods

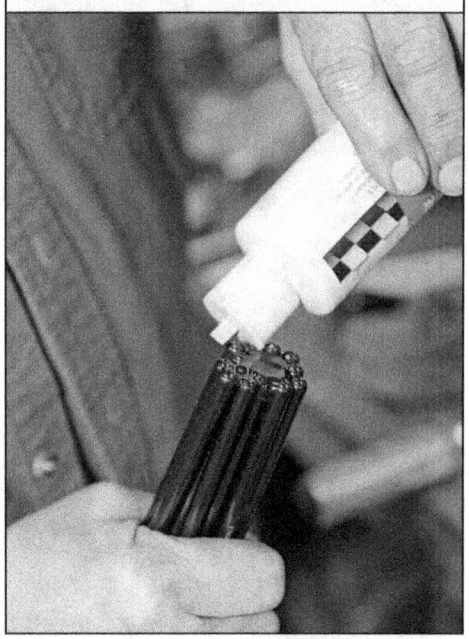

3 Zinc assembly lube is dripped on all the top and bottom of all pushrods.

HOW TO BUILD MAX-PERFORMANCE CHEVY LT1/LT4 ENGINES

CHAPTER 7

Add Oil to Valve

4 A dab of oil on each valve does the trick.

Tighten Spider Gear

5 Tighten the spider gear, holding the lifter retainers in place.

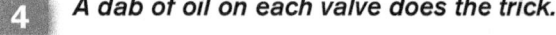
Rocker Arm Installation

Torque Rocker Studs

1 Rocker studs come next and are torqued down to 55 ft-lbs.

Install Exhaust Rocker Arm

2 *When the exhaust valve just barely begins to open, take the intake and run the nut down to zero lash. Then roll the motor over until the intake just closes. Install the exhaust rocker arm and take it down to zero lash. This procedure is used throughout the entire drivetrain. At this point you should be using this time to spin the crank shaft to notice any binds throughout the motor, i.e., camshaft ticks, connecting rod clearance, etc.*

Adjust Rocker Stud Alignment

3 *A quick check before you throw the valve covers on. You can use a flat bar to see if the rocker studs are fairly equal. They should be within one turn of each other.*

4 *One full turn of each rocker stud suffices. This is a quick way to make sure the rockers are properly snug and do not need to be fiddled with later.*

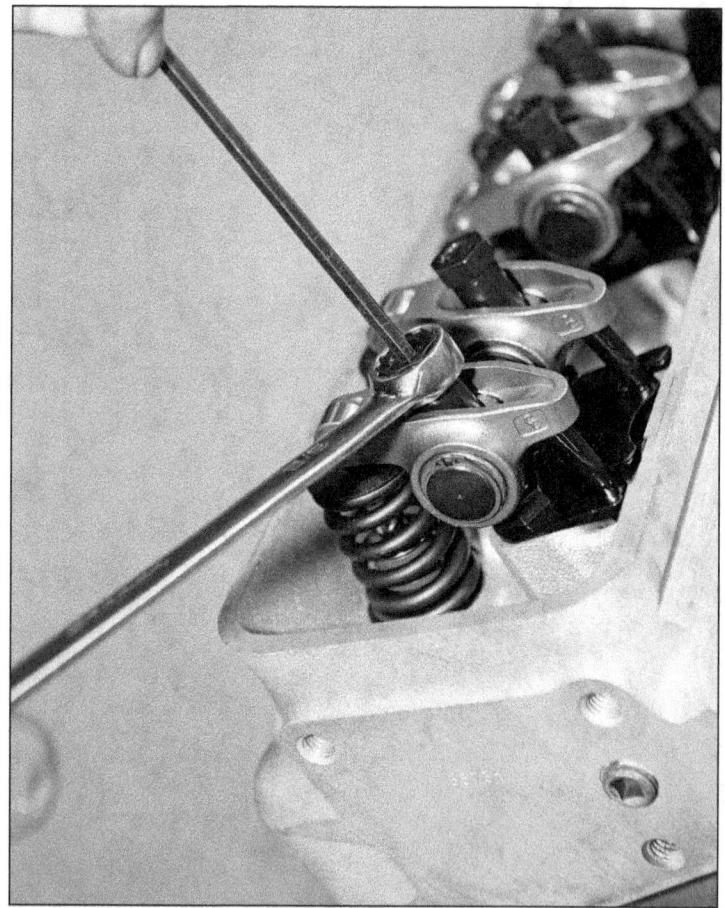

5 *Finally, snug the lock nut tight, back off the stud nut about a 1/16 turn, then tighten both stud and lock nut as one.*

Final Top End Assembly

Prime Oil Pump

1 Using a drill, the pump is primed prior to installing the gear drive to make sure the pump is functional and to pre-lube it prior to the first start up. This requires a special tool; or a modified distributor works just as well.

Inspect Oil Pump Drive Gear

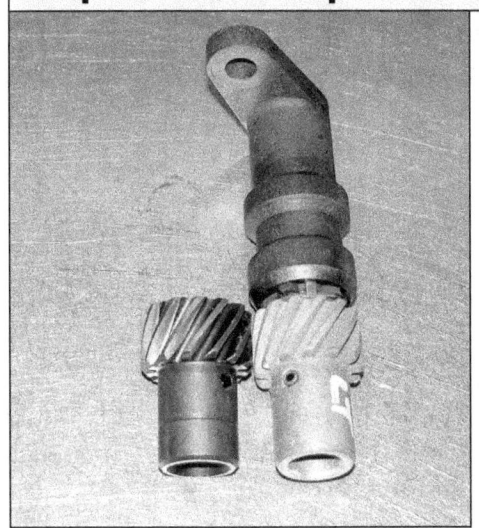

2 A new gear is cheap insurance. Our old one (left) has seen a lot of use and is worn down and needed to be replaced.

Install Oil Pump Drive Gear

3 Install the oil pump drive gear.

Intake Manifold Installation

Inspect Gaskets

1 Make sure your gaskets are LT-specific with no coolant holes.

Check Gasket Fit

2 Inspect throttle body gasket for alignment and fit.

Bolt the intake manifold into place. Install the throttle body, fuel rails, and injectors as shown.

Post Installation

Over the years, there have been several occasions when customers have called and said "…this motor feels kind of soft." Sure enough, I drive the car, and it is not as powerful as you would expect. So, where do you start? As always, begin with the basics. Listen to the engine when you start it up. By that, I mean, does it crank evenly? Crank it over and listen to hear if all cylinders are working. If you have trouble with this first test, pull one spark plug and then crank it over again. It will be very obvious that you have a dead cylinder, and you can compare this to your previous results.

For the next test, make sure all cylinders are producing heat. The inexpensive way to accomplish this is to spray something like WD-40, or even water, on each exhaust header pipe, then start the engine and ensure the moisture burns off evenly from all cylinders. This will surely reveal if any cylinders aren't working. A temperature gun is a much more accurate way of checking without the mess of spraying something on the pipes, but not everyone has one.

If all the cylinders are producing relatively even heat, you know the engine is functioning.

Next, check for full throttle travel. You'd be amazed how often things like a floor mat under the gas pedal, or the throttle linkage hitting the air cleaner, can limit a vehicle's engine performance. While it may seem silly lots of things get moved around and/or disassembled during an engine swap, so it's really not that odd for something to be out of place.

Next, check the engine's ignition timing. Some technicians grab the distributor to help when installing a new engine, and this kind of rough handling can really mess up the timing. Then, oddly enough, they never re-check the timing when the engine is fired. They expect it's been set correctly by the engine builder/tuner on the dyno (which is true, but by the time they tug and pull the distributor a few times during the engine installation, the distributor may have been moved). In the excitement of finishing the engine installation and getting it fired up for the first new ride, the timing does not get checked. Make sure you take the time to check the timing before you take a drive.

The next thing to check is the fuel pressure at idle, as well as throughout the run on a chassis dyno. If you have any suspicion that the air filter assembly is restricting the engine's power, now is the time to find out. Test without the filter in place to see how much of a difference it makes. If the filter setup is well-designed and clean, you should see no power loss and maybe even a power gain with the filter installed properly. If removing the air filter gains significant power, it's time for an upgrade to a proper high-performance unit.

Finally, make sure that the exhaust system is capable of supporting the power level you saw on the engine dyno. Look for things like double-wall pipe that may have collapsed, or catalytic converters that are old and probably clogged. Even some aftermarket upgrades (such as shorty headers) won't work well on a 600-hp engine. The engine has to breathe, so you must allow it to do so.

CHAPTER 8

DYNO RESULTS

The following is a series of engine dyno test results for a wide range of LT1/LT4 engines we've built here at the shop over the years. We've included all of the basic information, like displacement, cylinder head type, camshaft, etc., so you can compare our results to what you've got or what you're planning.

The purpose of sharing these dyno results is to help you plan your own project. Is it worth the extra money to get a stroker crankshaft? Well, the results shown will let you make that decision. We've learned the LT1/LT4 engines absolutely benefit from additional displacement, and stroker cranks are popular upgrades around here.

These dyno sheets represent twenty years of testing the LT1, including many equipped with the Mini Ram intake manifold we developed in-house. We introduced this at the 1990 SEMA show (for the traditional Gen 1 small-block Chevy) and adapted it for use with the LT1/LT4 soon afterward. It's proven to be a well-rounded high-performance design that still fits under the hood of most factory LT1/LT4-equipped vehicles. We're pretty proud of it. If you want a serious LT1, it's worthy of consideration, as you'll see.

Most of these dyno tests were run on 91-octane gasoline. These are primarily the kind of street/strip and track day engines typical enthusiasts want, which is why they've been chosen to share here. As long as first-rate parts and hardware are used in conjunction with these combinations, these types of engine will provide many years of enjoyment.

It's not uncommon for us to get a phone call from customers many years later, or to run into them at an event somewhere, and to hear them say, "You built an engine for me twenty years ago, and it still runs like new!" That is always gratifying to hear, and if you follow the parameters we've laid out in the engines on the following pages, you'll probably be able to enjoy similar results.

DYNO RESULTS

Build #1: Craig Nyhus 383-ci LT1

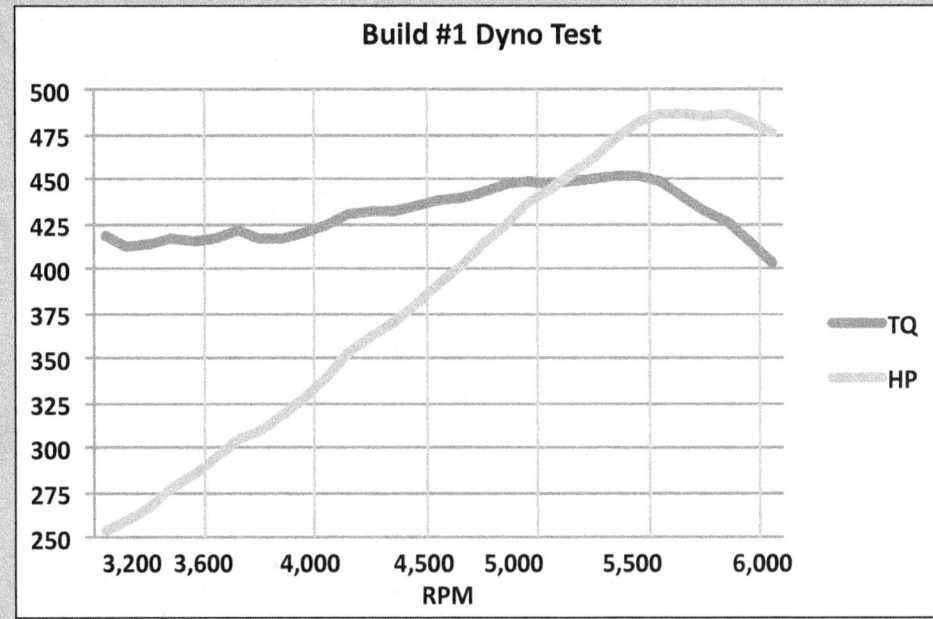

RPM	TQ	HP
3,200	418.2	254.0
3,300	413.0	259.5
3,400	413.5	267.7
3,500	417.9	278.5
3,600	416.4	285.4
3,700	417.7	294.3
3,800	421.1	304.7
3,900	416.9	309.6
4,000	417.9	318.3
4,100	420.5	328.3
4,200	425.1	340.0
4,300	431.0	352.9
4,400	432.0	362.6
4,500	432.1	370.2
4,600	435.0	381.0
4,700	438.3	392.2
4,800	439.9	402.0
4,900	443.2	413.5
5,000	446.8	425.4
5,100	449.2	436.2
5,200	448.2	443.8
5,300	449.3	453.4
5,400	450.6	463.3
5,500	**452.4**	473.8
5,600	452.4	482.4
5,700	449.3	**487.6**
5,800	440.4	486.4
5,900	432.6	486.0
6,000	425.9	486.6
6,100	415.8	482.9
6,200	403.3	476.1

Displacement	383 ci	**Oil Pan**	Canton road race
Block	GM, 4-bolt, .030 over	**Throttle Body**	TPIS, 52 mm
		Crankshaft	Callies, 3.75
Pistons	SRP, PN 139628	**Timing Chain**	Cloyes True Roller
Camshaft	TPIS ZZ409 hydraulic roller	**Intake**	GM LT1
		Ignition	Optispark
Rods	Scat ICR5700	**Compression Ratio**	11:1
Heads	GM LT1, CNC ported		

This is a mild street, strip, and track-day combination for use with pump gas. It boasts TPIS hand-ported cylinder heads, a 52-mm TPIS throttle body, and a ZZ409 camshaft.

The car is a 1995 Pontiac Firehawk with a factory T56 6-speed manual transmission. With more than 400 ft-lbs of torque available from as low as 3,000 rpm, a steady torque rise to a 452 ft-lbs maximum, and a power peak of 487 hp, this engine makes a very drivable track car that can still be used every day.

This build was done April 2007 and has seen many track days since. This combination consistently delivers freeway fuel economy between 20 and 25 mpg. The 383 runs just fine on mid-grade (89 octane) gasoline for light street-commuter duty. The owner fills it with pump premium (91 octane) for use on track days. It makes 16 inches of vacuum at idle and is a great example of a true street engine that's completely capable of part-time track duty on weekends.

Build #2: Dan Napoleone 383-ci LT4

Build #2 Dyno Test

RPM	TQ	HP
2,500	387.1	184.3
2,600	390.0	193.0
2,700	394.6	202.8
2,800	405.8	216.3
2,900	413.2	228.2
3,000	418.4	239.0
3,100	418.4	247.0
3,200	417.1	254.1
3,300	416.2	261.5
3,400	415.8	269.2
3,500	415.3	276.8
3,600	415.4	285.4
3,700	419.7	295.7
3,800	420.1	304.0
3,900	432.7	321.3
4,000	436.8	332.7
4,100	437.8	341.8
4,200	446.3	356.9
4,300	448.4	367.1
4,400	453.5	379.9
4,500	452.8	388.0
4,600	458.7	401.8
4,700	459.6	411.3
4,800	460.4	420.8
4,900	462.0	431.0
5,000	**462.5**	440.3
5,100	458.0	444.7
5,200	458.3	453.8
5,300	457.3	461.5
5,400	455.7	468.5
5,500	450.4	471.7
5,600	448.2	477.8
5,700	437.5	474.8
5,800	432.8	478.0
5,900	427.1	479.8
6,000	420.5	480.4
6,100	415.0	**482.0**
6,200	404.1	477.1
6,300	392.3	470.6
6,400	384.7	468.8

Displacement	383 ci	**Heads**	GM LT4, ported
Block	GM, 4-bolt, .030 over	**Oil pan**	Champ, Corvette
		Throttle body	TPIS, 52 mm
Pistons	ICON 80IC734, .030 over	**Crankshaft**	Howards 4340, 3.750 stroke
Camshaft	TPIS ZZ409	**Timing Chain**	GM high-performance billet roller
Intake/Exhaust (degrees)	226/226		
Lift (inches) .050		**Intake**	LT4
Intake/Exhaust Valve Lift (inches)	.520/.520	**Ignition**	Optipark with MSD
Centerline (degrees)	112	**Compression Ratio**	11:1
Rods	Scat, 6.000		

This build is very similar to Build #1, with the one major difference being cylinder heads. This one started with a set of factory LT4 castings, which have larger volume intake ports than Build #1's LT1 units. We then CNC ported the LT4 heads to improve flow capability even further. As a result, the larger port volume gives a little fatter torque curve.

This build was done in March 2011. Unfortunately, we have lost track of this customer so no follow-up information is available.

DYNO RESULTS

Build #3: Gary Rudolf 355 LT1

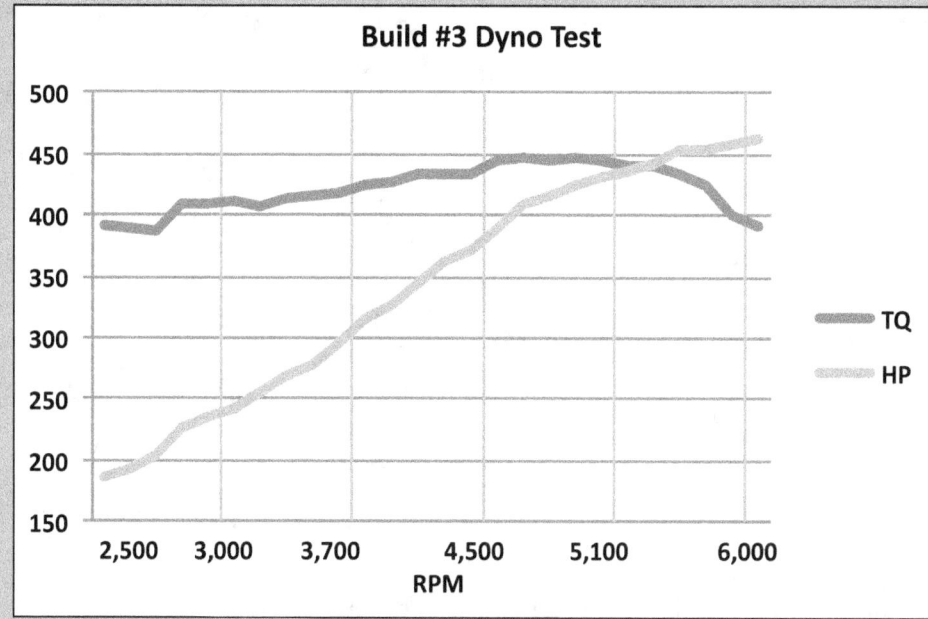

RPM	TQ	HP
2500	391.0	186.1
2600	390.3	193.2
2700	387.1	204.1
2900	410.5	226.7
3000	410.4	234.4
3100	410.8	242.5
3300	407.6	256.1
3400	414.2	268.2
3500	416.7	277.7
3700	418.8	295.0
3900	425.9	316.2
4000	428.3	326.2
4300	433.4	345.8
4400	432.9	362.7
4500	434.0	371.0
4600	445.2	390.0
4800	448.3	409.7
4900	445.7	415.8
5000	**447.2**	425.7
5100	444.9	432.0
5200	441.1	436.7
5300	439.9	443.9
5500	434.1	454.6
5600	424.8	453.0
6000	401.3	458.5
6200	392.4	**463.2**
6300	380.8	456.7

Displacement	355 ci	Rods	Scat I-beam, ICR 6.000
Block	LT1		
Pistons	SRP 138087, .030 over	Heads	GM LT1, CNC ported
Camshaft	ZZ-9	Oil pan	Champ
Intake/Exhaust (degrees)	212/226	Throttle Body	TPIS, 52 mm with TPIS Airfoil
Lift (inches)	.050	Crankshaft	GM stock stroke
Intake/Exhaust Valve Lift (inches)	.483/.520	Timing Chain	Cloyes billet roller
		Intake	GM LT1
Centerline (degrees)	112	Ignition	Optispark with MSD
		Compression Ratio	10.2:1

This is a 355-ci LT1 with our famous ZZ-9 camshaft. The stock heads have been CNC ported as well. This little horse pulls quite hard and is very impressive for its size. The power rise through the RPM range is linear and predictable, delivering smooth power throughout. This engine should provide lots of fun at an autocross or road course.

The owner's first comment when asked about the engine's power was, "It's fun!" We believe him.

Build #4: Buck Benziger 402-ci LT1

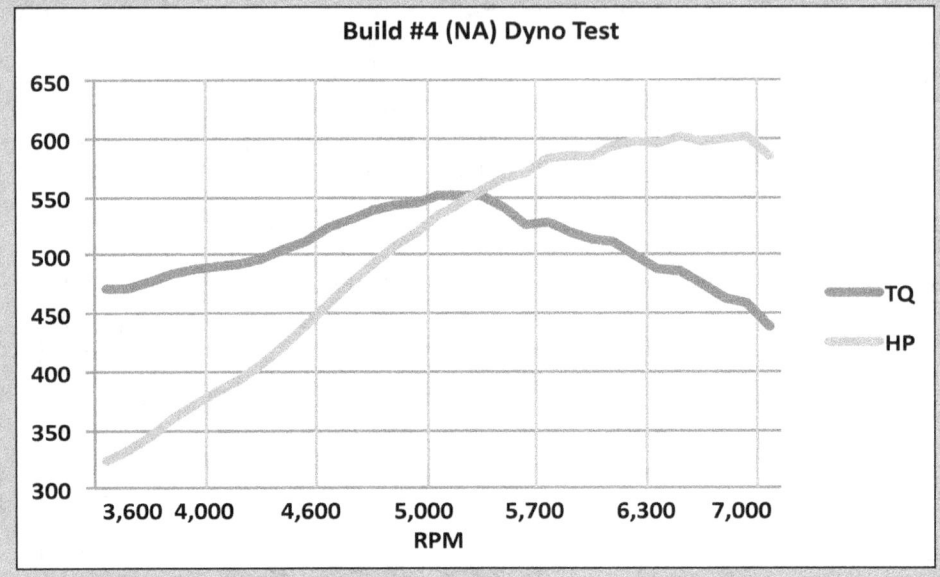

Displacement	402 ci, NO/2 test
Block	GM, cast 4-bolt with studs
Pistons	Ross, .060 over, therma and friction coatings
Camshaft	TPIS custom grind, solid roller
Intake/Exhaust (degrees)	258/266
Lift (inches)	.050
Intake/Exhaust Valve Lift (inches)	.640/.630
Centerline (degrees)	108
Rods	Lunati Pro Billet
Heads	AFR LT-4, 210 cc, full port
Oil Pan	Canton drag race
Throttle Body	TPIS 58 mm
Crankshaft	Callies Stealth
Timing Chain	Cloyes single-chain
Intake	Hogan sheet-metal with direct-port NOS
Ignition	Optispark GM with MSD 6AL with TPIS
Compression Ratio	11.8:1

RPM	TQ	HP
3,600	471.8	323.4
3,700	472.2	332.7
3,800	477.7	345.6
3,900	483.5	359.0
4,000	488.4	372.0
4,100	489.6	382.2
4,200	491.8	393.3
4,300	496.7	406.7
4,400	504.5	422.7
4,500	512.1	438.8
4,600	523.2	458.2
4,700	531.3	475.5
4,800	537.8	491.5
4,900	543.8	507.4
5,000	545.7	519.5
5,100	551.0	535.1
5,200	**551.3**	545.8
5,300	550.6	555.6
5,400	543.9	559.2
5,500	540.7	566.2
5,600	532.3	567.6
5,700	525.7	570.5
5,800	527.4	582.4
5,900	520.3	584.5
6,000	513.0	586.1
6,100	510.8	593.3
6,200	502.7	593.4
6,300	498.7	598.2
6,400	488.6	595.4
6,500	486.2	601.7
6,600	474.8	596.7
6,700	467.5	596.4
6,800	463.0	599.5
6,900	458.8	**602.8**
7,000	438.6	584.6

This is the big daddy LT1, making 602 normally aspirated horsepower! With a shot of nitrous, we saw 958 hp. The power was still heading upward and might have bumped 1,000 horses with a few hundred more RPM. This was a very nice engine, from top to bottom. Starting with the Hogan intake feeding a set of Air Flow Research (AFR) cylinder heads with an intake port volume of 210 cc; perfect for this displacement in this RPM band.

Benziger is building a tube frame chassis with a later-model (mid 1990s) Caprice body for drag racing. We have seen it and his workmanship is first rate. This engine will test it; that's for certain.

DYNO RESULTS

Build #4: Buck Benziger 402-ci LT1

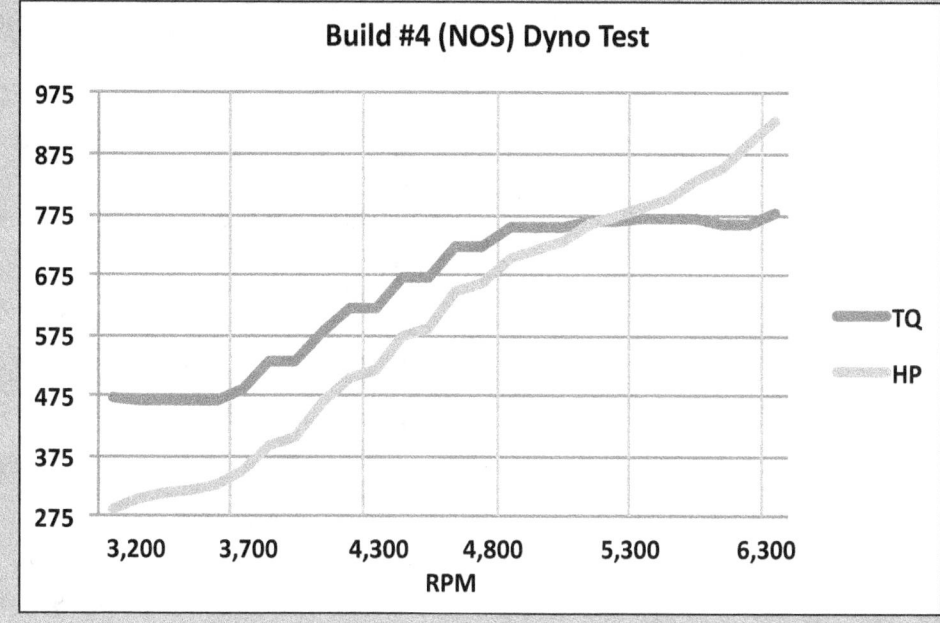

RPM	TQ	HP
3,200	471.2	287.1
3,300	463.5	302.2
3,400	466.8	302.2
3,500	467.4	311.5
3,600	467.4	320.4
3,700	467.5	329.4
3,800	485.1	351.0
3,900	531.4	394.6
4,000	531.5	404.8
4,100	581.3	453.8
4,200	581.4	464.9
4,300	617.9	505.9
4,400	618.0	517.7
4,500	670.2	574.2
4,600	670.3	587.1
4,700	722.4	646.5
4,800	722.4	660.2
4,900	753.1	702.6
5,000	753.2	717.1
5,100	753.3	731.5
5,200	764.3	756.7
5,300	764.4	771.4
5,400	766.2	787.8
5,500	766.3	802.5
5,600	767.5	818.4
5,700	767.6	833.1
5,800	767.7	847.8
5,900	759.1	852.8
6,000	755.3	862.9
6,100	758.3	880.7
6,200	758.4	895.3
6,300	777.1	932.2
6,400	**786.8**	**958.8**

Displacement	402 ci, NO/2 test	Rods	Lunati Pro Billet
Block	GM, cast 4-bolt with studs	Heads	AFR LT-4, 210 cc, full port
Pistons	Ross, .060 over, therma and friction coatings	Oil Pan	Canton drag race
		Throttle Body	TPIS 58 mm
		Crankshaft	Callies Stealth
Camshaft	TPIS custom grind, solid roller	Timing Chain	Cloyes single-chain
		Intake	Hogan sheet-metal with direct-port NOS
Intake/Exhaust (degrees)	258/266		
Lift (inches)	.050	Ignition	Optispark GM with MSD 6AL with TPIS
Intake/Exhaust Valve Lift (inches)	.640/.630		
Centerline (degrees)	108	Compression Ratio	11.8:1

The combination of the Hogan intake that was plumbed for nitrous makes this LT one stout Chevy. The nitrous shot was 300 hp.

Build #5: Ryan Custodio 355 LT1 Supercharged

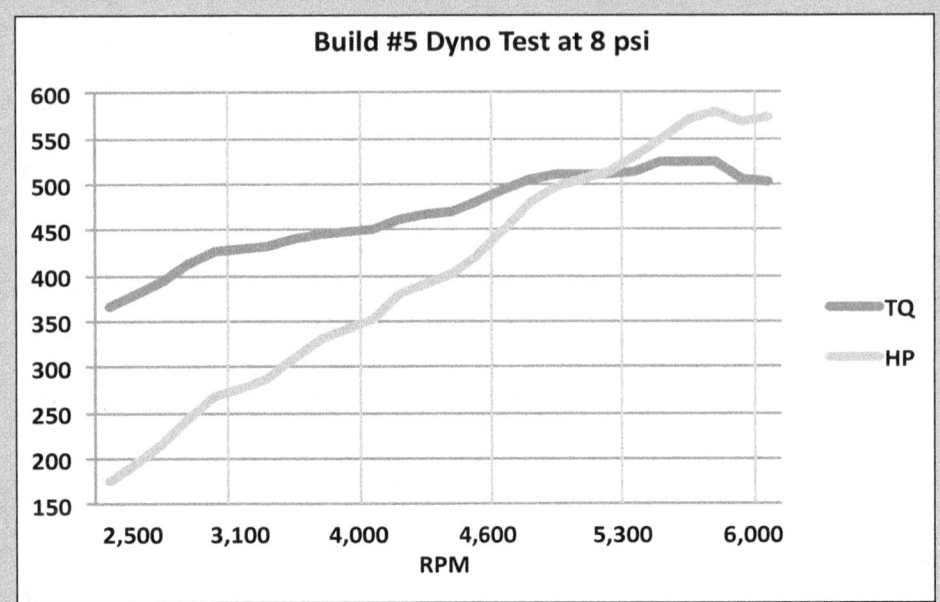

RPM	TQ	HP
2,500	366.3	174.4
2,600	372.2	184.3
2,700	379.6	195.1
2,800	388.0	206.9
2,900	392.5	216.7
3,000	405.6	231.7
3,100	412.7	243.6
3,200	419.3	255.5
3,3,00	426.8	268.2
3,400	428.9	277.7
3,500	432.5	288.2
3,600	436.2	299.0
3,700	439.9	309.9
3,800	441.7	319.6
3,900	445.2	330.6
4,000	447.5	340.8
4,100	451.6	352.5
4,200	454.6	363.5
4,300	462.7	378.8
4,4,00	467.7	391.8
4,500	469.8	402.5
4,600	481.4	421.6
4,700	487.7	436.4
4,800	493.8	451.3
4,900	500.2	466.7
5,000	505.7	481.4
5,100	511.3	496.5
5,200	510.8	505.7
5,300	509.7	514.4
5,400	514.5	529.0
5,5,00	523.9	548.6
5,600	524.4	559.1
5,700	**526.0**	570.9
5,800	525.5	**580.3**
5,900	506.9	569.4
6,000	502.4	574.0

Displacement 355 ci
Block LT1 with billet cap
Pistons Diamond, .030 over, TPIS coated
Camshaft TPIS ZZ409
  Intake/Exhaust 226/226
  (degrees)
  Lift (inches) .050
  Intake/Exhaust .520/.520
  Valve Lift (inches)
  Centerline (degrees) 112
Rods Manley Sportsman, 6-inch
Heads TPIS, ported LT1
Oil Pan Stock
Throttle Body 52 mm
Crankshaft Stock
Timing Chain Cloyes
Intake GM LT1
Ignition GM Optispark with MSD 6 al
Compression Ratio 9.1:1 Vortech supercharger at 8 psi

This engine was designed to live in a supercharged environment from the start. The main bearing caps have been upgraded to much stronger billet versions, the connecting rods are forged-steel aftermarket units, the forged pistons have been coated with a thermal barrier, and all of the critical fasteners were upgraded from the factory hardware to high-quality ARP products. But, the stock block, crank, and heads were used, so you can see there is plenty of potential in them when they are properly prepared.

Running at 8 psi provided both a baseline to plan for the increased boost and also offers a nice, conservative setup for street use. This 8-psi arrangement would be fine in traffic or on a long trip like the Power Tour. Because the LT1 engine design cools the heads first, the factory cooling system should prove perfectly adequate with this setup as well. The Vortech supercharger doesn't add significant boost until after 3,000 rpm, so the engine remains quite civilized in the lower RPM ranges where most street and freeway driving happens. But, from 3,000 rpm up, there are substantial power gains and the engine's power is really on display.

DYNO RESULTS

Build #5: Ryan Custodio 355 LT1 Supercharged

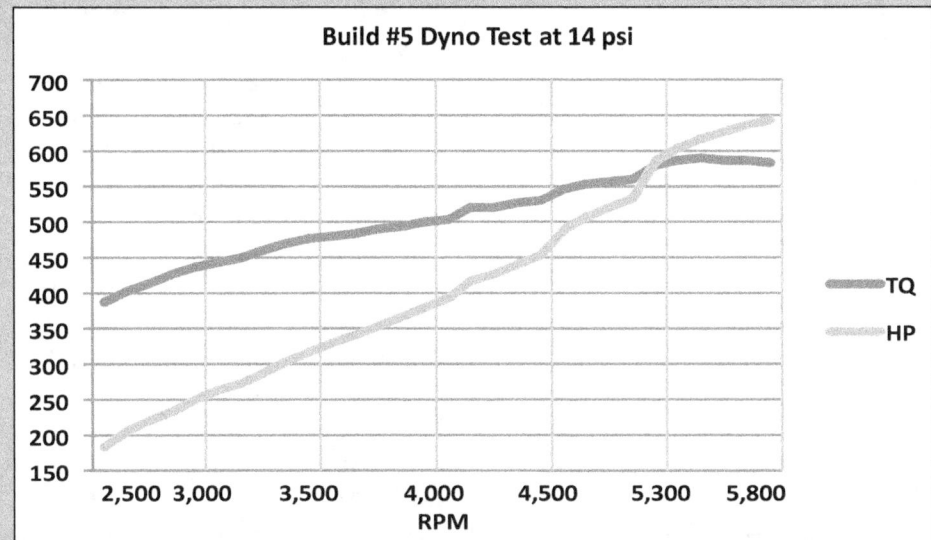

RPM	TQ	HP
2,500	388.4	184.9
2,600	396.0	196.0
2,700	404.0	207.7
2,800	414.3	220.9
2,900	426.8	235.7
3,000	438.1	250.2
3,100	445.4	262.9
3,200	451.5	275.1
3,300	460.7	289.5
3,400	471.7	305.4
3,500	476.6	317.6
3,600	481.2	329.8
3,700	485.9	342.2
3,800	490.8	355.1
3,900	495.7	368.1
4,000	500.6	381.3
4,100	505.3	394.5
4,200	520.7	416.4
4,300	520.7	426.3
4,400	527.6	442.0
4,500	531.5	455.4
4,600	539.0	472.1
4,700	547.1	489.6
4,800	554.3	506.6
4,900	558.2	520.8
5,000	562.5	535.5
5,100	562.5	546.2
5,200	578.6	572.9
5,300	581.5	586.8
5,400	589.1	605.7
5,500	**591.7**	619.6
5,600	588.1	627.1
5,700	586.7	636.7
5,800	584.7	**645.7**

Displacement 355 ci
Block LT1 with billet cap
Pistons Diamond, .030 over, TPIS coated
Camshaft TPIS ZZ409
  Intake/Exhaust 226/226
  (degrees)
  Lift (inches) .050
  Intake/Exhaust .520/.520
  Valve Lift (inches)
  Centerline (degrees) 112
Rods Manley Sportsman, 6-inch
Heads TPIS, ported LT1
Oil Pan Stock
Throttle Body 52 mm
Crankshaft Stock
Timing Chain Cloyes
Intake GM LT1
Ignition GM Optispark with MSD 6 al
Compression Ratio 9.1:1 Vortech supercharger at 14 psi

Now, this is the exact same engine with just a pulley change (and the required reprogramming to keep the fuel and ignition in tune with the needs of the engine). While your eyes probably went right to the peak numbers (which are quite impressive), please take a moment to look over the entire RPM range. Note how low the RPM levels are where this engine starts making big power. This much boost generates a fair amount of heat, so an upgrade to a more efficient radiator is recommended. An intercooler wouldn't be a bad idea either (if there is sufficient clearance under the hood to accommodate it) and would add even more power by cooling the incoming charge.

This engine lives in a Corvette, and it has spent many enjoyable hours on the track, being pushed to its limits on a regular basis. It has also proven to be very drivable on the street, where the owner has enjoyed it on many nice summer days. The overall impression of this engine is truly a Jekyll/Hyde split personality. It's tame and smooth around town at low RPM, but if you open it up, it becomes a 645-hp monster.

Build #6: Jim Hall 402-ci LT1

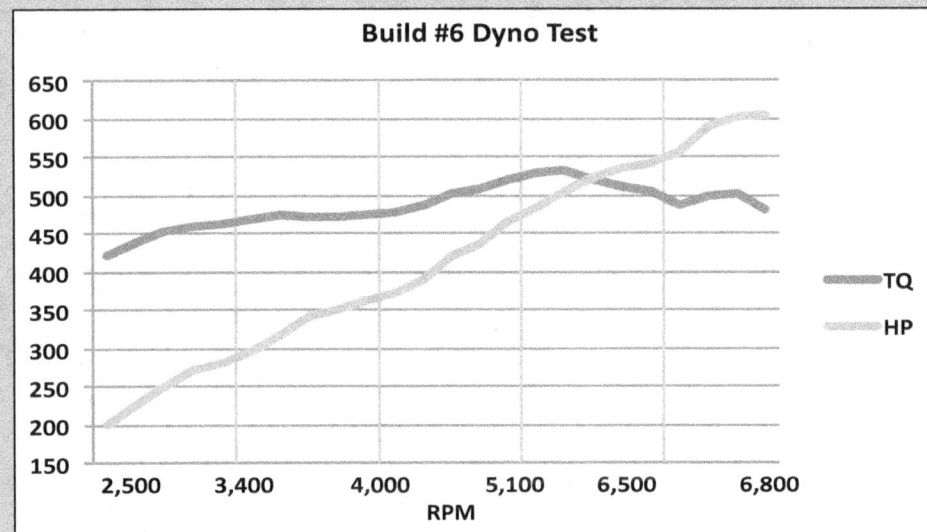

Displacement	402 ci
Block	GM with splayed caps
Pistons	Diamond, .060 over
Camshaft	234l solid roller
Intake/Exhaust (degrees)	242/242
Lift (inches)	.050
Intake/Exhaust Valve Lift (inches)	.572/.572
Centerline (degrees)	112
Rods	Manley Sportsmaster, 6 inch
Heads	AFR, 203 cc
Oil Pan	Canton road race
Throttle Body	58 mm
Crankshaft	Callies Magnum
Timing Chain	Cloyes
Intake	GM LT1
Ignition	Optispark with MSD 6 AL
Compression Ratio	11.5:1
Injectors	27 pounds

RPM	TQ	HP
2,500	422.2	201.0
2,600	433.6	214.7
2,700	440.5	226.5
2,800	449.1	239.4
2,900	454.0	250.7
3,000	454.0	259.3
3,100	460.6	271.9
3,200	464.2	282.8
3,300	469.6	295.1
3,400	474.9	307.4
3,500	476.4	317.5
3,600	474.0	324.9
3,700	469.5	330.8
3,800	473.1	342.3
3,900	471.7	350.3
4,000	475.4	362.1
4,100	477.2	372.5
4,200	488.4	390.6
4,300	490.7	401.8
4,400	501.8	420.4
4,500	507.7	435.0
4,600	518.3	454.0
4,700	521.8	467.0
4,800	528.9	483.4
4,900	528.2	492.8
5,000	**532.4**	506.9
5,100	531.8	516.4
5,200	527.5	522.3
5,300	520.4	525.2
5,400	514.9	529.4
5,500	511.9	536.1
5,600	507.2	540.8
5,700	504.5	547.5
5,800	495.5	547.2
5,900	492.8	553.6
6,000	488.9	558.5
6,100	507.2	589.1
6,200	499.6	589.8
6,300	501.5	601.6
6,400	493.7	601.6
6,500	483.8	598.8
6,600	481.9	605.6
6,700	475.1	**606.1**
6,800	459.8	595.3

The owner of this engine works at TPIS. This engine is a collection of new and used parts. As you can see, the results are very good.

This engine has suprisingly good driving manners and many "experts" said we weren't going to be able to tune it properly with the cam we selected. But, they were proven wrong. The owner put more than 8,000 road racing/track day miles on it once it was installed in his 1994 Camaro 1LE, backed with a 6-speed manual transmission and a 3.42:1 gear, and it never skipped a beat. He and his wife also drove the car from Minneapolis, Minnesota, to the Black Hills of South Dakota and managed 18 mpg with it on the 2,000-mile trip.

The car boasts big torque everywhere in the RPM range, and it loves to reel in new ZO6 Corvettes, Twin Turbo Porsche 911s, and many other unsuspecting victims. It's a killer road race engine, but also has great street manners considering its power and the fact it runs exclusively on pump gas.

DYNO RESULTS

Build #7: John Schaefer 383

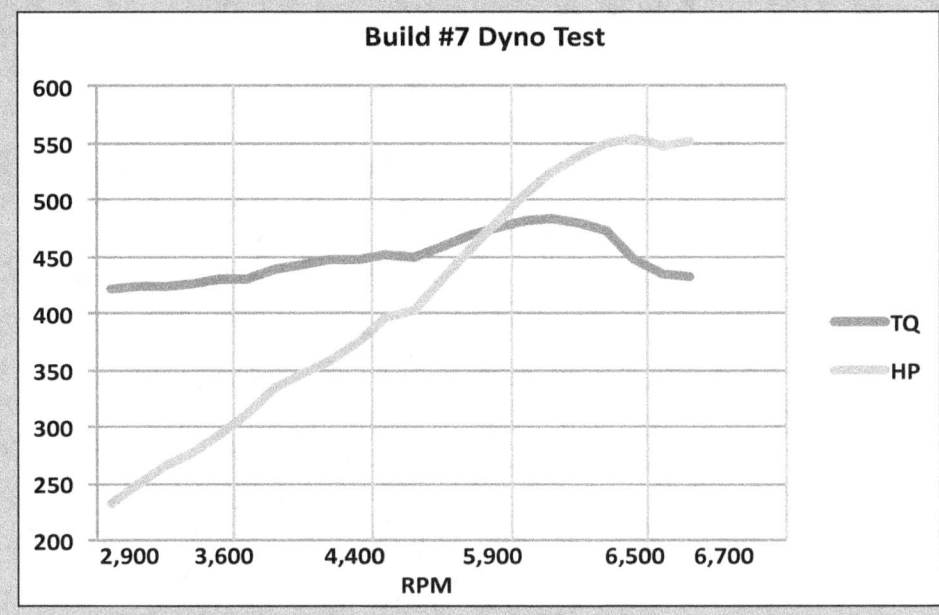

RPM	TQ	HP
2,900	420.8	232.4
3,000	425.2	242.9
3,100	423.2	249.8
3,200	422.2	257.2
3,300	423.6	266.2
3,400	425.9	275.7
3,500	429.1	286.0
3,600	429.7	294.2
3,700	429.1	302.3
3,800	429.7	310.9
3,900	433.4	321.8
4,000	438.8	334.2
4,100	443.8	346.5
4,200	446.4	357.0
4,300	447.6	366.5
4,400	447.5	374.9
4,500	450.7	386.2
4,600	451.1	395.1
4,700	450.5	403.2
4,800	452.1	413.2
4,900	458.7	428.0
5,000	466.5	444.1
5,100	469.2	455.6
5,200	474.8	470.1
5,300	474.8	479.1
5,400	476.5	489.9
5,500	481.3	504.0
5,600	485.6	517.8
5,700	483.4	524.6
5,800	**485.7**	536.4
5,900	479.3	538.4
6,000	475.5	543.2
6,100	473.1	549.5
6,200	465.5	549.5
6,300	458.0	549.4
6,400	449.5	547.8
6,500	447.2	**553.5**
6,600	435.0	547.8
6,700	432.9	552.3

Displacement	383 ci		Rods	GM
Block	GM with splayed caps		Heads	GM LT1, TPIS CNC ported
Pistons	Diamond, .030 over		Oil Pan	Canton road race
Camshaft	TPIS ZZ409		Throttle Body	TPIS, 52 mm
Intake/Exhaust (degrees)	226/226		Crankshaft	GM, cast iron
			Timing Chain	Cloyes
Lift (inches)	.050		Intake	TPIS Mini-Ram 2 LT
Intake/Exhaust Valve Lift (inches)	.520/.520		Ignition	MSD
Centerline (degrees)	112		Compression Ratio	11.2:1

In this test we saw 5- to 10-hp gains by switching to a Mini Ram. On this engine we saw gains on the order of 21 hp and 12 ft-lbs. These kind of gains are very satisfying.

Build #8: Ron Bilyeu 409

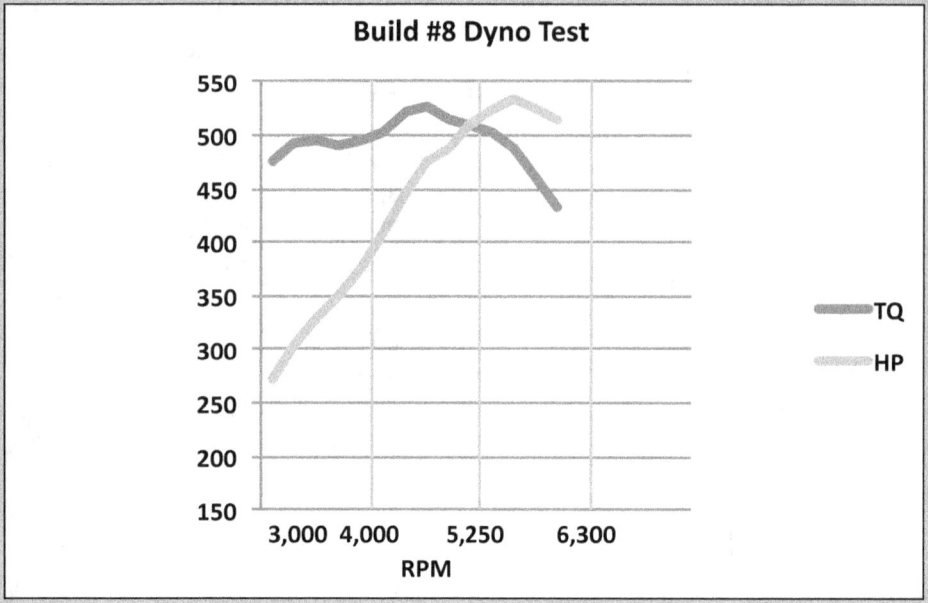

RPM	TQ	HP
3,000	475.5	271.6
3,250	491.7	304.3
3,500	494.5	329.5
3,750	491.1	350.7
4,000	495.4	377.3
4,250	503.2	407.2
4,500	521.3	446.7
4,750	**526.2**	475.9
5,000	513.5	488.9
5,250	510.2	510.0
5,500	501.6	525.3
5,750	487.4	**533.6**
6,000	459.9	525.4
6,250	433.0	515.3

Displacement	409 ci	**Heads**	GM LT1, ported by TPIS in-house
Block	LT1		
Pistons	Diamond, 4.100	**Oil Pan**	Champ
Camshaft	TPIS custom grind	**Throttle Body**	58 mm
Intake/Exhaust (degrees)	239/239	**Crankshaft**	Callies, 3.875 stroke
Lift (inches) .050		**Timing Chain**	Cloyes
Intake/Exhaust Valve Lift (inches)	.558/.558	**Intake**	GM LT1
		Ignition	MSD
Centerline (degrees)	112	**Compression Ratio**	11.2:1
Rods	Manley billet	**Rockers**	1.52

This build was done so long ago that our dyno collected data every 250 rpm; today we collect every 100 rpm.

Build #9: Golen Engine Service 396-ci LT1

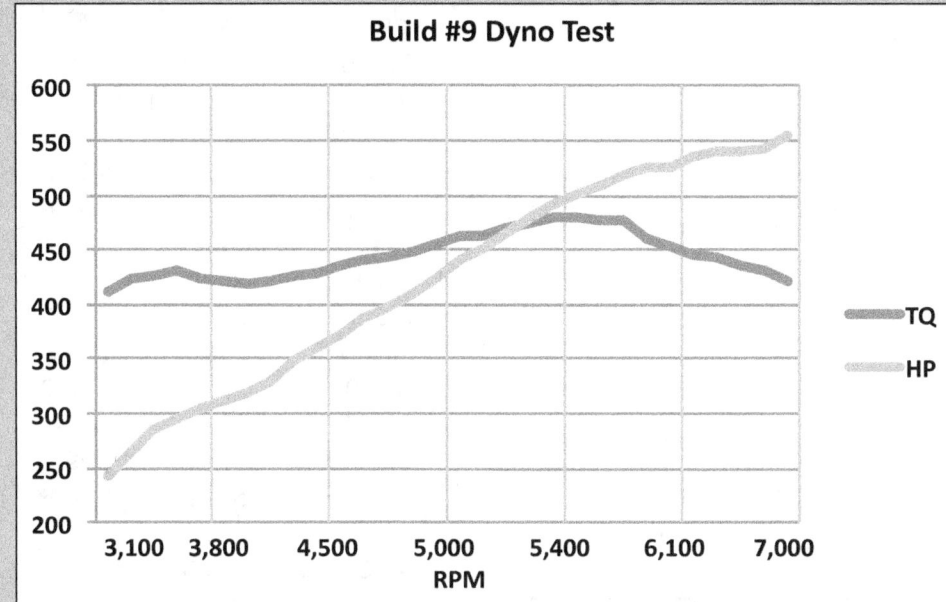

Displacement	396 ci	Throttle Body	TPIS, 58 mm
Block	LT1	Crankshaft	Callies
Pistons	Diamond	Timing Chain	Cloyes
Camshaft	Comp Cams, solid roller, 07-000-9	Intake	GM LT1
		Ignition	Optispark with MSD
Rods	Manley Pro I-Beam	Compression Ratio	11.5:1
Heads	AFR 210		
Oil Pan	Canton		

This engine is a 396-ci LT1 designed to run to a 7,000-rpm redline while still making a large torque number down low. A Comp Cams solid roller (PN 07-000-9) was used for this application.

This engine went into a 1990s-era Caprice, which is a large, heavy car. All we can say is that this tank really hauls.

RPM	TQ	HP
3,100	411.7	243.0
3,200	416.5	253.8
3,300	424.4	266.7
3,400	426.6	276.2
3,500	427.5	284.9
3,600	431.1	295.5
3,700	425.1	299.5
3,800	422.9	306.0
3,900	421.9	313.3
4,000	420.2	320.0
4,100	422.3	329.7
4,200	424.3	339.3
4,300	426.3	349.0
4,400	429.4	359.7
4,500	436.2	373.7
4,600	441.5	386.7
4,700	443.2	396.6
4,800	448.5	409.9
4,900	454.4	423.9
5,000	462.5	440.3
5,100	463.5	450.2
5,200	470.6	465.9
5,300	474.8	479.1
5,400	478.7	492.2
5,500	**479.2**	501.8
5,600	476.5	508.1
5,700	478.4	519.2
5,800	469.9	518.9
5,900	463.1	520.2
6,000	459.9	525.4
6,100	452.0	525.0
6,200	446.9	527.6
6,300	446.6	535.7
6,400	443.7	540.7
6,500	435.8	539.4
6,600	431.8	542.6
6,700	432.4	551.6
6,800	426.6	552.3
6,900	421.5	553.8
7,000	419.4	**559.0**

Build #10: TPIS Intake Test Motor

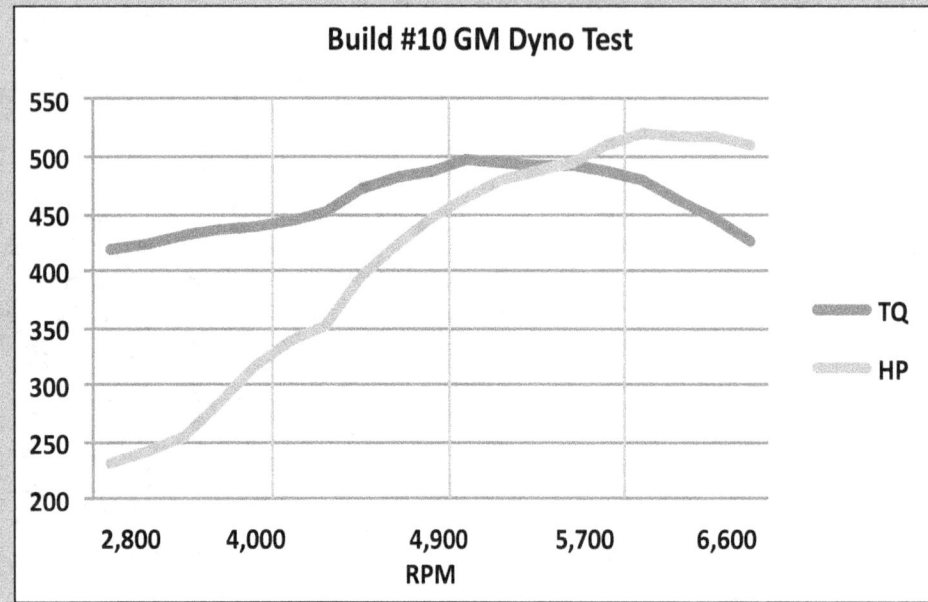

RPM	TQ	HP
2,800	413.9	220.7
2,900	418.7	231.2
3,000	422.6	241.4
3,100	430.8	254.3
3,200	432.7	263.6
3,300	433.5	272.4
3,400	435.7	282.1
3,500	434.0	289.2
3,600	434.3	297.7
3,700	433.9	305.7
3,800	438.1	317.0
3,900	444.0	329.7
4,000	444.6	338.6
4,100	450.7	351.8
4,200	453.6	362.7
4,300	460.0	376.6
4,400	471.0	394.6
4,500	478.1	409.6
4,600	482.1	422.3
4,700	485.3	434.3
4,800	487.7	445.7
4,900	**497.1**	463.8
5,000	494.6	470.9
5,100	493.9	479.6
5,200	491.9	487.0
5,300	491.0	495.5
5,400	494.1	508.0
5,500	487.6	510.6
5,600	478.0	509.7
5,700	478.5	**519.3**
5,800	469.5	518.5
5,900	461.1	518.0
6,100	445.2	517.1
6,200	434.5	512.9
6,300	426.2	511.2
6,400	418.1	509.5
6,500	408.2	505.2
6,600	399.0	501.4

Displacement 383 ci
Block LT1 with splayed bolts
Pistons Diamond, .030 over
Camshaft ZZ-X
Rods Manley, 6.000
Heads AFR
Oil Pan Canton road race
Throttle Body TPIS, 58 mm
Crankshaft Scat, 3.750
Timing Chain Cloyes
Intake GM LT
Ignition Optispark with MSD
Compression Ratio 11.2:1

This is a two-part intake manifold comparison test between a factory LT1 intake and an Edelbrock aftermarket intake. Both of the intakes were port-matched to the cylinder heads, and each intake showed advantages at different RPM levels.

In the first test, the factory LT1 manifold showed its torque-producing capability by making 497 ft-lbs at 4,900 rpm. This was the highest torque number produced by either intake manifold, and shows that the ported factory intake is a great choice for dedicated street driving using a basic 383-inch LT1-based package like this with a ZZ-X camshaft. The 519-hp figure at 5,700 rpm is certainly respectable, and places this engine configuration's redline just under 6,000 rpm, which is relatively low. This means the engine's internal parts won't be stressed by high RPM, and the engine should be able to provide many years of reliable service using this intake/cylinder head and camshaft combination.

DYNO RESULTS

Build #10: TPIS Intake Test Motor

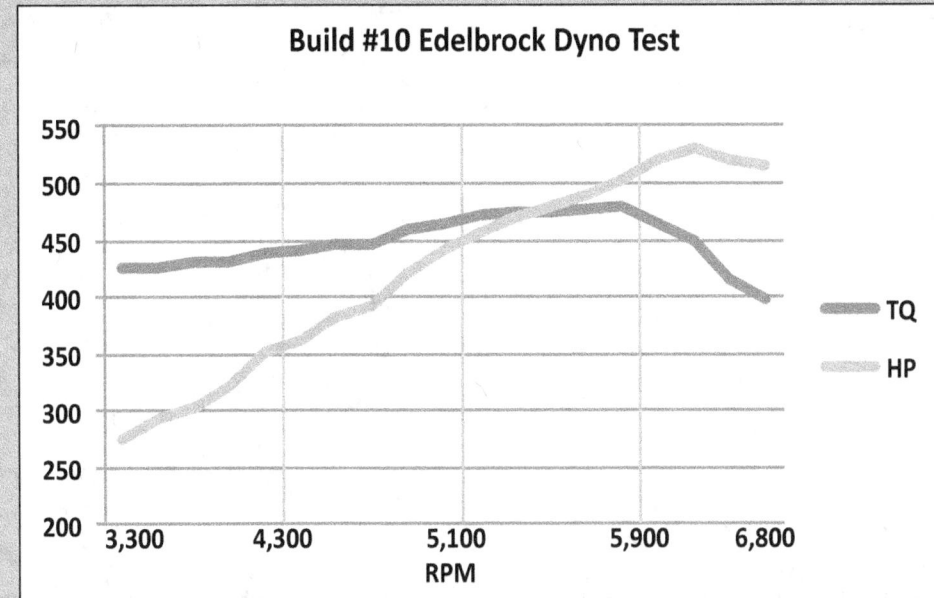

RPM	TQ	HP
3,300	423.6	266.2
3,400	424.7	274.9
3,500	427.6	285.0
3,600	426.6	292.4
3,700	430.7	303.4
3,800	433.2	313.4
3,900	432.0	320.8
4,000	435.2	331.5
4,100	437.5	351.5
4,200	438.5	350.7
4,300	441.9	361.8
4,400	446.0	373.6
4,500	445.3	381.5
4,600	447.1	391.6
4,700	447.4	400.4
4,800	459.9	420.3
4,900	461.7	430.8
5,000	464.2	441.9
5,100	471.1	457.5
5,200	473.3	468.6
5,300	474.9	479.2
5,400	476.7	490.1
5,500	**479.8**	502.5
5,600	477.7	509.4
5,700	473.0	513.3
5,800	468.9	517.8
5,900	463.6	520.8
6,200	449.9	**531.1**
6,500	421.0	521.0
6,600	414.6	521.0
6,700	403.3	514.5
6,800	397.8	515.0

Displacement	383 ci		**Throttle Body**	TPIS, 58 mm
Block	LT1 with splayed bolts		**Crankshaft**	Scat, 3.750
			Timing Chain	Cloyes
Pistons	Diamond, .030 over		**Intake**	Edelbrock LT
			Ignition	Optispark with MSD
Camshaft	ZZ-X		**Compression Ratio**	11.2:1
Rods	Manley, 6.000			
Heads	AFR			
Oil Pan	Canton road race			

In the second test, the Edelbrock intake manifold made 479 ft-lbs of torque at 5,500 rpm, but horsepower moved up to 531 at 6,200 rpm. The engine liked the additional airflow past 6,000 rpm, but had to sacrifice 20 ft-lbs of peak torque to get it. For a car that sees occasional track time at either the dragstrip or the road course, that extra high RPM power would be appreciated. Over 6,000 rpm, better parts are required, particularly valvesprings and rocker arms. This is especially true if the driver spends a lot of time in those higher RPM ranges, which can happen on road courses.

CHAPTER 8

Build #11: Mooney LT1 392

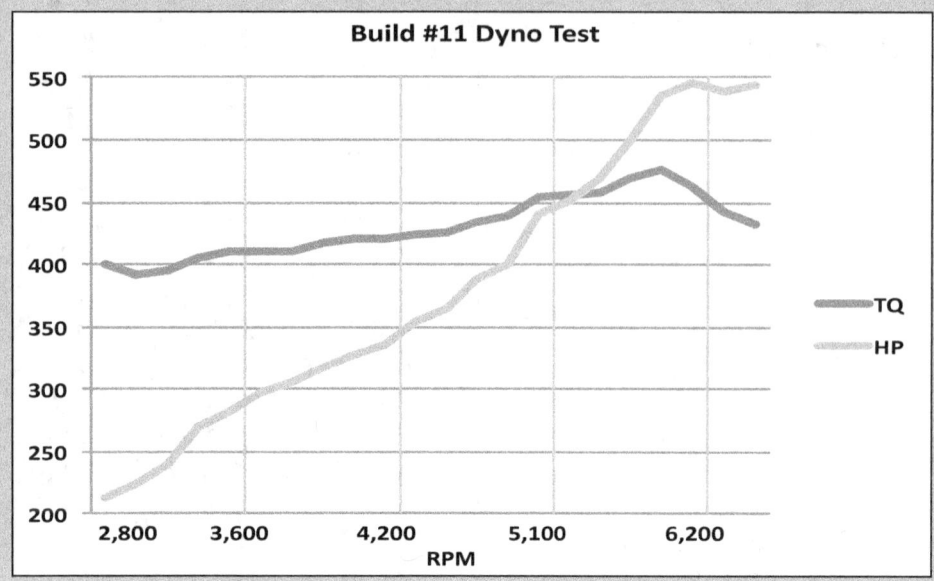

RPM	TQ	HP
2,800	399.8	213.1
2,900	385.2	218.2
3,000	391.3	223.5
3,100	392.3	231.6
3,200	394.4	240.3
3,300	398.8	250.6
3,400	404.6	261.9
3,500	405.6	270.3
3,600	410.2	281.2
3,700	410.7	289.3
3,800	411.0	297.4
3,900	410.4	304.8
4,000	416.6	317.3
4,100	419.9	327.8
4,200	420.9	336.6
4,300	423.1	346.4
4,400	423.6	354.9
4,500	426.3	365.3
4,600	431.2	377.7
4,700	434.5	388.8
4,800	438.7	400.9
4,900	443.0	413.3
5,000	445.8	424.4
5,100	453.6	440.5
5,200	455.6	451.1
5,300	457.1	461.3
5,400	457.3	470.2
5,500	461.1	482.9
5,600	468.7	499.8
5,700	467.8	507.7
5,800	471.4	520.6
5,900	**476.2**	535.0
6,000	470.5	537.5
6,100	465.7	540.9
6,200	462.5	**546.0**
6,300	453.1	543.5
6,400	441.9	538.5
6,500	437.6	541.6
6,600	432.9	544.0

Displacement 392 ci
Block LT1
Pistons Diamond 24259
Camshaft TPIS ZZ-X hydraulic roller
  Intake/Exhaust (degrees) 239/239
  Lift (inches) .050
  Intake/Exhaust Valve Lift (inches) .558/.558
  Centerline (degrees) 112
Rods Oliver, 5.850
Heads Modified LT1
Oil Pan Canton road race, 7-quart
Throttle Body 58 mm
Crankshaft Lunati CM
Timing Chain Cloyes early LT1
Intake LT1
Ignition Stock
Compression Ratio 11:1

This engine lives in a 1993 Camaro purchased new by Mike Mooney in western South Dakota. It's a hardtop that came with the optional "M28" 6-speed manual transmission that included a 2.73:1 rear gear ratio. That ended up being an important option for Mike's ultimate purpose of building a fourth-generation Camaro with the highest possible top-speed potential.

Mike started off with some of the typical easy bolt-on parts, but in his quest for top speed he added a Vortech supercharger kit. It was faster, as Mike was able to achieve 219.7 mph.

He also gained cooling problems and other issues that seemed to come along with forced-induction power. He decided to ditch the blower and have the engine rebuilt with higher compression for trouble-free, low-maintenance cruising on the occasional track day. For this build, he turned to TPIS.

They reused the factory LT heads and chose a ZZ-X cam, which is a hydraulic roller with 239 degrees of duration at .050 inch and .558 inch of lift on a 112-degree centerline. A set of Oliver forged connecting rods and a Lunati 3.75-inch stroke crankshaft (along with a Canton road race pan) rounded out the first TPIS build of this engine. After a short period of time, Mike was back for more (see page 125).

Build #12: Todd Danielson/Mooney LT1 396

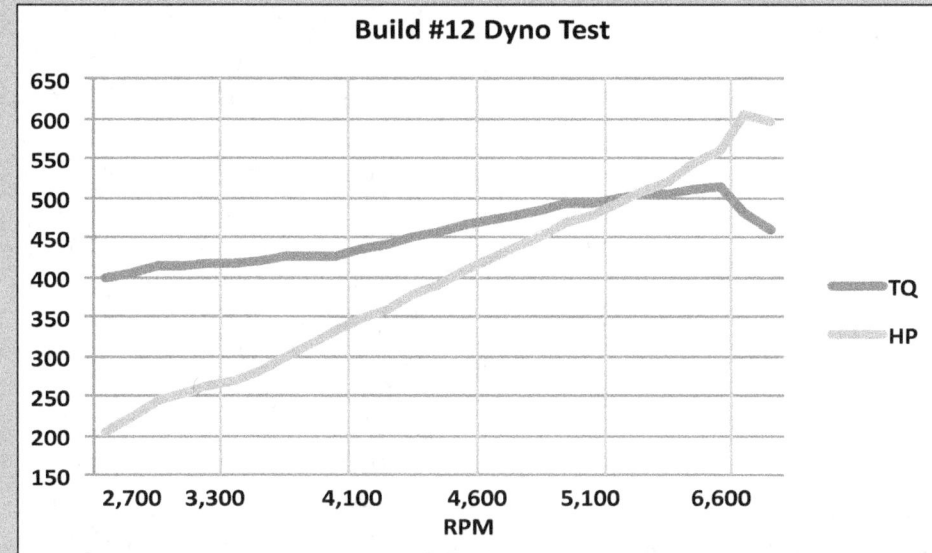

Displacement	396 ci
Block	LT1 with billet caps
Pistons	Ross, 4.060
Camshaft	TPIS solid roller
Intake/Exhaust (degrees)	259/268
Lift (inches) .050 Intake/Exhaust Valve Lift (inches)	.640/.630
Centerline (degrees)	112
Rods	Oliver, 5.850
Heads	AFR 210
Oil Pan	Canton road race, 7 quart
Throttle Body	58 mm
Crankshaft	Lunati CM
Timing Chain	Cloyes early LT1
Intake	LT1
Ignition	Optispark with MSD
Compression Ratio	11.8:1

This second TPIS rebuild included another overbore (another .020 inch to 396 ci), a change in piston design (including a revised skirt shape and a larger dome to bump compression up to 11.8:1) with a different Total Seal ring package, Jesel shaft-mount rockers, a nasty solid-roller camshaft, and a pair of Air Flow Research (AFR) 210-cc cylinder heads, ported to TPIS specifications. This new combination was good for 606 peak horsepower on the engine dyno.

The fuel injector size was 36 pounds, which is right at the max for 550 hp. So, 40 lb/hr units were installed and the programing was revised to compensate for the new changes. As you can see, the result is a streetable 600 hp. Since this build, the owner switched to E85 fuel, larger injectors, and has reprogrammed the ECU for use with the new fuel.

The Camaro is now owned by Todd Danielson of Track Time Motorsports, and is the shop's official track car. It still does get out on the street occasionally, but most of its run time is spent at Brainerd International Raceway during open track days.

RPM	TQ	HP
2,700	398.6	204.9
2,800	402.0	214.3
2,900	404.7	223.5
3,000	410.0	234.2
3,100	413.8	244.2
3,200	415.8	253.3
3,300	417.7	262.5
3,400	417.0	270.0
3,500	421.2	280.7
3,600	426.3	292.2
3,700	426.4	300.4
3,800	427.7	309.5
3,900	425.7	316.1
4,000	424.3	323.2
4,100	427.5	333.7
4,200	436.0	348.7
4,300	441.0	361.1
4,400	450.1	377.1
4,500	457.5	392.0
4,600	466.3	408.4
4,700	472.5	422.8
4,800	479.0	437.8
4,900	483.0	450.6
5,000	494.0	470.3
5,100	493.7	479.4
5,200	499.2	394.3
5,300	504.7	509.3
5,400	506.6	520.9
5,500	514.4	538.7
5,600	512.1	546.0
5,700	**515.6**	559.6
5,800	515.2	569.0
5,900	510.1	573.0
6,000	502.6	574.2
6,100	507.2	589.1
6,200	499.6	589.8
6,300	501.5	601.6
6,400	493.7	601.6
6,500	483.8	598.8
6,600	481.9	605.6
6,700	475.1	**606.1**
6,800	459.8	595.3

Build #13: 368 for Bonneville Salt Flats

Build #13 Dyno Test

RPM	TQ	HP
4,000	386.3	294.2
4,100	390.9	305.2
4,200	396.9	317.4
4,300	399.5	327.1
4,400	402.4	337.1
4,500	404.2	346.3
4,600	411.4	360.3
4,700	414.1	370.6
4,800	420.5	384.3
4,900	427.3	398.7
5,000	429.6	409.0
5,100	430.2	417.7
5,200	435.4	431.1
5,300	449.7	453.8
5,400	454.2	467.0
5,500	462.8	484.7
5,600	469.8	500.9
5,700	**470.1**	510.2
5,800	468.4	517.3
5,900	467.9	525.6
6,000	465.7	532.0
6,100	460.1	534.4
6,200	458.1	541.1
6,300	452.3	542.6
6,400	450.2	548.6
6,500	442.8	548.0
6,6,00	440.0	552.9
6,700	439.1	560.2
6,800	434.4	562.4
6,900	426.1	559.8
7,000	419.3	558.9
7,100	416.2	562.6
7,200	410.9	563.3
7,300	406.7	565.3
7,400	401.7	**566.0**
7,500	385.6	550.6

Displacement	368 ci
Block	GM LT1 splayed bolts and straps
Pistons	Diamond, 4.100 coated
Camshaft	TPIS custom
Intake/Exhaust (degrees)	260/265
Lift (inches)	.050
Intake/Exhaust Valve Lift (inches)	.685/.684
Centerline (degrees)	108
Rods	Manley, 6.125, forged
Heads	Air Flow Research
Intake Valve	2.080 inches
Exhaust Valve	1.625 inches
Chamber	59 cc
Oil Pan	Canton road race
Throttle Body	TPIS, 58 mm
Crankshaft	GM cast, normalized, gas nitrided
Timing Chain	Cloyes double-row chain
Intake	TPIS Mini-Ram 2
Ignition	Motec M8 programmable
Compression Ratio	12.2:1

This build was for an attempt to get my (Myron's) SCCA World Challenge 1994 Camaro to run 200 mph at Bonneville. Then, my brother went to Bonneville and his car came back with the chassis full of salt. So, for now I'm going to stick it in the car for some local salt-free open track days.

APPENDIX

Cylinder Head Flow Data

Intake

Lift (inch)	.100	.200	.300	.400	.500	.600	.700
TPIS LT-1 409	62	134	203	233	247	258	—
Intake Port Volume: 189 cc							
Chamber Volume: 53.3 cc							
L-98 Stock	60	115	161	184	196	199	—
Intake Port Volume: 161 cc							
Chamber Volume: 56 cc							
L-98 Stage 1	60	127	190	233	254	254	—
Intake Port Volume: 189 cc							
Chamber Volume: 58 cc							
LT-1 Stock	58	113	167	203	212	—	—
Intake Port Volume: 169 cc							
Chamber Volume: 54 cc							
LT-1 Stage 1	63	129	192	238	260	258	—
Intake Port Volume: 188 cc							
Chamber Volume: 53 cc							
LT-4 Stock	56	119	179	218	241	232	—
Intake Port Volume: 199 cc							
Chamber Volume: 53 cc							
LT-4 Stage 1	56	123	196	235	261	276	282
Intake Port Volume: 212 cc							
Chamber Volume: 55.5 cc							

Below are heads that we did not personally test:

Lift (inch)	.100	.200	.300	.400	.500	.600	.700
AFR 190 cc	—	129	195	240	260	262	—
AFR LT4 195-cc Comp 2.02	135	201	249	275	280	—	—
Lingenfelter	197	236	252	261	—	—	—
GTP Stage II LT4 2.02	66.9	137.5	193.5	246.3	265.6	280.2	—

Exhaust

Lift (inch)	.100	.200	.300	.400	.500	.600	.700
TPIS LT-1 409	52	119	153	174	185	192	—
Total Intake/Exhaust Flow Ratio: 78.5%							
L-98 Stock	47	103	133	155	165	—	—
Total Intake/Exhaust Flow Ratio: 83%							
L-98 Stage 1	54	97	132	171	196	198	—
Total Intake/Exhaust Flow Ratio: 77%							
LT-1 Stock	47	97	133	152	160	—	—
Total Intake/Exhaust Flow Ratio: 79.4%							
LT-1 Stage 1	53	107	138	171	185	182	—
Total Intake/Exhaust Flow Ratio: 76%							
LT-4 Stock	47	102	140	164	176	182	—
Total Intake/Exhaust Flow Ratio: 79%							
LT-4 Stage 1	47	106	146	168	187	196	204
Total Intake/Exhaust Flow Ratio: 78.7%							

Below are heads that we did not personally test:

Lift (inch)	.100	.200	.300	.400	.500	.600	.700
AFR 190 cc	—	108	156	178	190	194	—
AFR LT4 195-cc Comp 2.02	110	157	180	195	208	—	—
Lingenfelter	151	185	190	207	—	—	—
GTP Stage II LT4 2.02	56.7	112	148.4	183.7	198.9	208.1	—

Source Guide

Air Flow Research
28611 W. Industry Dr.
Valencia, CA 91355
877-892-8844
www.airflowresearch.com

Callies
901 S. Union St.
Fostoria, OH 44830
419-435-2711
www.callies.com

Cam Motion
2092 Dallas Dr.
Baton Rouge, LA 70806
225-926-6110
www.cammotion.com

Canton Racing Products
232 Branford Rd.
North Branford, CT 06471
203-481-9460
www.cantonracingproducts.com

Comp Cams
3406 Democrat Rd.
Memphis, TN 38118
800-999-0853
www.compcams.com

Dart Machinery
353 Oliver Dr.
Troy MI, 48084
248-362-1188
www.dartheads.com

Diamond Pistons
23003 Diamond Dr.
Clinton, MI 48035
877-552-2112
www.diamondpists.net

EFI Connection
814-566-0946
www.eficonnection.com

Jesel
1985 Cedar Bridge Ave., Suite 2
Lakewood, NJ 08701
792-901-1800
www.jesel.com

Manley Performance Products
1960 Swarthmore Ave.
Lakewood, NJ 08701
732-905-3366
www.manleyperformance.com

Total Seal
22642 N. 15th Ave.
Phoenix, AZ 85027
800-874-2753
www.totalseal.com

TPIS
4255 Creek Rd.
Chaska, MN 55318
952-448-6021
www.tpis.com

www.ingramcontent.com/pod-product-compliance
Lightning Source LLC
Chambersburg PA
CBHW051415070526
44584CB00023B/3435